5-

The GREAT AMERICAN PIE Book

RECIPES FOR THE SWEET AND THE SAVORY FROM CHICKEN POTPIE TO PEACH BLUEBERRY

JUDITH CHOATE ❖ PHOTOGRAPHY BY MICHAEL GRAND

Simon & Schuster

London Sydney New York Tokyo Toronto Singapore

A KENAN BOOK

Copyright © 1992 Kenan Books, Inc.

Text copyright Judith Choate

THE GREAT AMERICAN PIE BOOK was first published in 1984,
copyright © Yankee Publishing Incorporated.

 Simon & Schuster
Simon & Schuster Building
Rockefeller Center
1230 Avenue of the Americas
New York, New York 10020

SIMON & SCHUSTER and colophon are registered trademarks of Simon & Schuster Inc.

THE GREAT AMERICAN PIE BOOK
was prepared and produced by
Kenan Books, Inc.
15 West 26th Street
New York, New York 10010

Editor: Sharon Kalman
Art Director: Robert W. Kosturko
Designer: Susan E. Livingston
Photography Editor: Christopher C. Bain
All interior photography © Michael Grand 1992
Food styling by Heather Swain
Prop styling by Heidi Carlson

1 3 5 7 9 10 8 6 4 2

Library of Congress Cataloging-in-Publication Data

Choate, Judith
    The great American pie book / Judith Choate.
        p.   cm.—(American kitchen classics)
    Includes index.
    ISBN 0-671-73550-0
    1. Pies. I. Title. II. Series
TX773.C526   1991
641.8′652—dc20

91-27276
CIP

Typeset by Miller & Debel, Inc.
Color separation by United South Sea Graphic Art Co., Ltd.
Printed and bound in Hong Kong by Leefung-Asco, Ltd.

Dedicated

with love to
My Grandmother Gilmour
My Mom
My Aunt Frances
My Auntie Blossom
My Aunt Annie
and Huey

Table of

Contents

INTRODUCTION

Pie! As American as Apple Pie!. . . Pie in the Sky!. . . A piece of Pie!. . . As easy as Pie!

This traditional food has meant something warm, comforting, and delicious as long as cooks have been combining ingredients between pastry crusts. Pies are so much a part of our dining heritage that early kitchens had cupboards called pie safes to keep freshly baked dinners or desserts under cover.

In more recent times, pies have usually been thought of as desserts. And in this book, I include terrific ones to tempt you. However, featured are recipes for the main-course pies that were developed for a unique bakery in New York City called MOM.

Raised on my mother's and aunt's meat and dessert pies, I had long been aware of the goodness of home-made pies. And as a working mother, I knew that there was a need for quality "homemade" food for easy cooking. What better than pies to fill the bill—fully prepared, nutritious meals in minutes.

It took one full year for the idea of a pie shop to germinate. The main problem was translating my mom's "pinch of ____" and "handful of ____" into precise measurements. Although I had always considered myself a competent cook, I would call on my mother to make holiday pies or my children's favorite chicken potpie. In a pinch, I bought already prepared frozen pastry shells; like many other cooks, I had given up trying to make a successful crust. Besides, it was easier to call Mom! If I was to develop a never-fail commercial product, however, I had to learn. Many arguments and a broken scale later, a perfect pastry recipe was developed.

The secret of success to the recipes in this book is the combination of high-quality fillings with high-quality crusts. The Flaky Pastry, originally based on my grandmother's recipe, is a typically American dough utilizing vegetable shortening, flour, salt, and water. It is light, flaky, and delicious, and you can learn how to make it and the other crust recipes successfully. I include directions for making pie crust by hand, electric mixer, and food processor.

Also included is a main-course pie that is everybody's favorite: Chicken (-In-Every-) Potpie. Consumers are tired of the skimpy ingredients, flour-leaden/laden sauces, and soggy products available in the freezer sections of most supermarkets, and they have welcomed a freshly made pie filled with chunks of chicken, potatoes, peas, carrots, and onions. Quality ingredients in a quality product. Basic, filling, nourishing, and tasty, it's easy to make and guaranteed to be a hit.

I have developed quiche recipes, too, because of their astounding popularity, and I give you a basic quiche recipe with many variations. You are limited only by what you have available in your cupboard or refrigerator.

Want an interesting hors d'oeuvre? Try empanadas or any version of a meat- or vegetable-filled pastry that can be made in advance, frozen, and reheated when you need it. Vegetarians will welcome the selection of pies using only vegetables or vegetables combined with cheese or eggs.

As popular as our main-course pies are, we have discovered that a great demand still exists for homemade dessert pies. Everyone, it seems, no matter how strict their diet, loves pie. No traditional holiday is complete without a pumpkin, mincemeat, squash, or, of course, apple pie. I include recipes for those as well as for other fruit pies, nut pies, cream, custard, and chocolate pies. There are double-crust pies and crumb-topped pies as well as whipped-cream or meringue-covered pies.

There are so many recipes included that you'll find you can make, eat, and enjoy pies no matter what time of the year. There's a selection of main-course and dessert pies that can be filled and frozen, unbaked, for future cooking, too. Just as we have in our retail store, you can always have a hearty dinner or luscious dessert on hand in your freezer. A great shortcut and a great help for any cook.

The recipes in this book come from many sources. Some evolved from my own experimentation, others are family favorites, but just as many have been generously given to me by friends and customers. I have loved learning new recipes, changing those I didn't like, enjoying those I did, and always finding new fillings to wrap in a pastry crust. No longer remembering what came from whom, I thank each person who has shared family pie secrets with me.

Chapter

GENERAL INFORMATION

One

USEFUL KITCHEN EQUIPMENT

The equipment you use to make pastry will depend on your personal preference.Except for a rolling pin, I have never used any of the equipment especially designed for pastry preparation. My equipment consists of the following items:

- Standard measuring cups and spoons
- Mixing bowl
- Two kitchen knives
- Fork for pricking or knife for design-piercing
- Oven thermometer
- Pastry wheel, pizza cutter, cookie cutter (only necessary for making lattice or other fancy tops)
- Cool, even surface to roll out dough
- Rolling pin (The selection is very personal. Feel is more important than material. If it rolls easily in your hands, moves with you— rather like a dancing partner—it's for you. Whatever type or size you prefer, use it lightly. Remember, you should not *push* the dough down, you should *roll* it out.)

If you would feel more comfortable or confident with a few more tools at hand, consider this additional equipment:

- Pastry blender
- Dough scraper
- Pie funnel (there are some charming animal-shaped ceramic funnels)
- Marble pastry board (some old kitchens and some new designer kitchens have permanent marble blocks built in for pastry-making)
- Pastry-cloth cover for rolling pin
- Baking weights (metal nuggets that are placed in the bottoms of pie shells to keep them from puffing up when they are baked without fillings)
- Cooling racks (those with legs will allow pies to cool faster)

All recipes in this book call for a 9-inch pie plate. For home use, I recommend those made of glass or ceramic. If you use disposable aluminum tins, be sure to place them on a cookie sheet to aid in browning the bottoms.

MAKING PERFECT PASTRY

Pastry has been a staple of kitchens for generations and it can easily be a staple of yours. There is absolutely no mystery to making perfect pastry, but there is definitely a lot of fear associated with it; so much, in fact, that some cooks will not even attempt it. If you follow these few simple rules, you will be able to successfully create flaky, light pastry.

1. Always use an easy hand when mixing and/or handling the dough. The more you handle it, the tougher the pastry will be.

2. Always follow the directions given with each pastry recipe. Do not improvise or substitute ingredients.

3. Always roll out the dough on a *cool* surface: marble, Formica, pastry board, etc. *Surface material* is *not* as important as *coolness* of the surface. French chefs generally recommend marble. I use the Formica top of my kitchen counters, rubbing the Formica with a bag of ice before rolling out the dough.

Pastry dough should be handled as little and as quickly as possible and should never be sticky. Hot, humid weather sometimes presents special problems, and if you are having difficulties, chill the dough for approximately half an hour before rolling it out.

Cool any cooked filling before pouring it into a pie shell unless you are going to bake the pie immediately. Otherwise, the hot filling will melt the pastry and result in an unattractive pie. And do not overfill a pie shell, for this causes spillover and creates a mess in the oven. If you have some filling left, pour it into any appropriate-size dish, lined with pastry if you desire, and bake with the pie.

INGREDIENTS

You may wonder how combining three simple ingredients—flour, shortening, and water—can produce flaky, melt-in-your-mouth pastry. Yet generations of cooks have used variations on these three basic pantry items to create full meals, great desserts, appetizers, and snacks. All pastry doughs, no matter what their origins, begin with these ingredients, but the ratio of one to another, the type of shortening used, and the addition of an egg yolk or sweetener or flavoring all affect the end product.

Traditional pastry requires all-purpose flour. Do not substitute any other type. In recipes that call for another kind of flour, the proportions of shortening and liquid have been adjusted for the type of flour used. Remember, the flour/shortening ratio sets the texture of the pastry.

Butter, margarine, vegetable shortening, or lard? Each makes a different type of pastry. Butter and margarine, which have more moisture than vege-table shortening or lard, may be used interchangeably. Taste will differ but the resulting texture of the pastry will be the same. It is preferable to use unsalted (sweet) butter or margarine. If you use salted, be sure to adjust the salt in the recipe. Butter makes the richest pastry.

Vegetable shortening or lard makes the flakiest pastry. Lard, of course, contributes a distinctive flavor, while vegetable shortening does not. They, too, may be used interchangeably. Taste and cholesterol count may determine which you choose. I almost always use vegetable shortening but do occasionally use lard to make pastry for meat pies. Whichever the shortening, never use it in either a frozen or overly warm state. If it is too hard, it will be difficult to work into the flour; too soft, it will break down more quickly than it should.

Cold or hot water? My cooking heritage says ice water. I have tried the hot-water method but have never been able to get an edible crust from it. I usually fill a cup with ice water and measure out of it. Many pastry recipes say "about" when giving water measurements and the less used the better! Why some days you use a full one-quarter cup and others a little bit less can only be determined by the kitchen witch.

MIXING AND HANDLING

Whether you mix your dough by hand or with an electric mixer or food processor, the steps required are the same. First, mix the flour and salt together. Second, blend this mixture with the shortening, and last, sprinkle in the liquid.

If mixing by hand, use two knives (working scissor-like) or a pastry blender and rapidly cut the shortening into the flour until the mixture resembles a coarse meal. The faster you work, the cooler the mixture will stay. Sprinkle the ice water, *a tablespoon* at a time, over the flour mixture, mixing quickly and easily with a fork. Mix in just enough water so the dough holds together when pressed lightly into a ball. (If the dough is sticky, you have added too much water. Refrigerate and use for bottom crusts.) The less you mix, the flakier and lighter the end result will be.

When working with an electric mixer, use the wire whip attachment first and then the dough hook. Follow the same procedure as by hand, using the wire whip to cut in the shortening and the dough hook to add liquid; flick the mixer off and on when blending. Work quickly!

I have also had excellent results using a food processor. Its speed makes incorporating the shortening and water a breeze. Follow the same procedure as by hand, but use the blade prescribed for pastry-making in your processor booklet. Mix the dough with a few quick on-off turns of the switch.

With clean, cool, dry hands form the dough into a ball. If your kitchen is warm, you may wish to wrap the dough in clear plastic wrap and refrigerate it for approximately 30 minutes to facilitate rolling out.

If you have never made pastry, rolling out the dough is where you may panic. Don't! Remember your light hand and proceed. Prepare the rolling-out surface by *lightly* coating it with flour. Divide the dough into equal portions and form each into a smooth ball, being careful not to over-work the dough. Take one ball and lightly press it onto the floured surface, using the heel of your hand to flatten. Smooth the edges as you go to prevent breakage when you roll out.

Lightly flour the rolling pin. Use quick, short strokes to roll dough from center out in every direction. Lift the rolling pin gently as you near the edge of the pastry to prevent breakage. Continue rolling out until you have an even circle ⅛ inch thick and about 2 inches wider than your pie plate. Lift the pastry circle by gently folding it in half over the rolling pin

and slip it, still folded, into pie plate. Unfold to cover the bottom of the pie plate and remove the rolling pin. Do not stretch dough or it will shrink when baked. If pastry tears, patch with left-over dough or pinch together. Do not overwork! Smooth pastry into pie plate with quick pressing movements. Make certain there are no holes that would allow pan juices to escape.

FOR BOTTOM SHELL ONLY

Press dough firmly against edge of plate. If shell is to be bottom of double-crust pie, leave excess pastry hanging over edge of plate until top crust is in place. Otherwise, turn under excess pastry and press gently to make a rim. Starting at edge opposite you, pinch dough between thumb and index finger around edge of pie at 1-inch intervals, forming a fluted

Roll dough from center out in every direction.

Lift the pastry by folding it in half over the rolling pin.

Smooth pastry into pie plate with quick pressing movements.

design. Keep turning pie as you work. You may leave pastry fluted or flatten edge slightly by pushing down with the tines of a fork. Be sure pressure on fork is downward and towards the center of pie. To prevent breakage and burning be sure edge is smooth and uniform.

FOR TOP CRUST

Roll out dough as described on page 16. Put filling into pastry-lined pie plate. Fold top crust in half over rolling pin, lift, and place over filling. Unfold to cover filling and attach to bottom crust by pressing together excess dough from bottom and top crusts. Fold pressed dough edge up and inward, making a rim around edge of pie. Starting at edge opposite you, pinch dough between thumb and index finger around edge of pie at

Pinch between the thumb and index finger to form a fluted design.

1-inch intervals, forming a fluted design. Keep turning pie as you work. The pastry can be left this way or you may then flatten edge slightly with a fork. Be sure pressure on fork is downward and towards the center of pie. Be sure edge is smooth and uniform to prevent breakage and burning.

There are several ways to finish the closed top crust so that steam is allowed to escape as the pie bakes. One is to pierce the top crust with fork tines. Another is to insert a ceramic pie funnel in the center of the filled, unbaked pie. A more decorative steam vent is a patterned opening. Before you place the top crust on the filled bottom, fold it in half and create a design on it by making small slashes with a kitchen knife.

FOR FANCY TOPS

It is easier to make a fancy top if you roll the dough slightly thicker than the normal ⅛ inch.

Lattice Top

Do not trim excess pastry from the bottom crust or fold it under to form rim. With a pastry wheel, cut one pastry lid into strips about ¼ inch to ½ inch wide. Using the longest strips for the center of the pie and working out from the center, lay half the strips horizontally across the pie ¾ inch apart. Working in the same manner, lay the remaining strips vertically across the pie. Strips may also be angled to form a diamond pattern. Trim off

ends of strips but do not trim bottom pastry. Turn bottom pastry edge up and over strip ends and press firmly down with a fork or crimp edge as described above.

Easy Woven Lattice Top

Do not trim excess pastry from bottom crust. Cut top crust into strips about ¼ inch to ½ inch wide. Take longest strip and lay it across the center of the pie horizontally. Take the next longest strip and lay it across the center of the first strip vertically, forming a cross. Take the next two longest strips and lay them horizontally on each side of the center cross, ¾ inch apart. Take two more strips and place them vertically on each side of center, ¾ inch apart. Continue in this manner until top is covered and seal as directed above.

For a tightly woven top, weave the individual strips one at a time.

Cut-Out Top

Prepare bottom and top as you would for a standard double-crust pie. Before you place the top crust on the pie, cut a design into it or cut a design out of it using cookie cutters. Carefully position on top of filling and crimp as described earlier.

Pattern Top

Use bottom shell that has the edges crimped. Roll out a pastry circle as you would for a top crust. Cut desired shapes from pastry circle using cookie cutters and place on top of filling. Do not leave too much open space or filling will dry out.

Extra Decorating

Pastry cut-outs or raised forms made from leftover pastry may be used to decorate the top crust of any pie. Make them by tracing around a simple item like a spoon, toy sailboat, holiday symbol, etc. Or you can trace simple designs by laying a pattern directly on the rolled-out pastry and pricking around the edges of it with a fork. Then cut the design out of the pastry with a small paring knife and attach it to the top crust with a bit of water or egg wash.

Raised forms can be made in the following manner:

• **Bow** Cut a 12-inch-long strip from leftover rolled-out pastry. Fold it into a bow shape. Trim the loose ends into an inverted V-shape and place a small ball of dough in the center of the bow to give the appearance of a knot.

• **Flower** Cut eight small circles (about 1-inch-to 1½-inch-diameter) from leftover rolled-out pastry. Using two of the circles for the center, join together to make a small, almost closed top. Pinch bottom of circles together. Holding the bottom, turn center gradually, adding other circles as you go to resemble petals. Pinch bottom, yet pull out petals to form a solid flower. Trim off any unsightly edges. Make stem and leaves out of remaining dough if desired. Always dampen the underside of trim with a bit of water or egg wash to make it stick to the top crust.

You can be as creative as you like. Here, cut-out moons and stars decorate the pie.

An alternating flower and four-leaf clover pattern.

Here, the dough is braided to create an unusual trim.

You may want to give your pastry an extra glow by coating it with egg wash. This can be done on any pastry-topped pie by using a pastry brush to coat the top with a wash made by whisking one egg with two tablespoons cool water. For dessert pies, you can add sparkle by sprinkling the egg wash with granulated sugar or granulated sugar-cinnamon mix. Either of these methods is great to use on pies for bake sales or for show.

Frequently, you will have scraps of pastry remaining after you have made your pie. Never throw them away! Even a small amount can be used for appetizers or snacks. My childhood favorite was "crispies," which my mother made by rolling out the leftover pastry, spreading it with soft butter, sprinkling with cinnamon and sugar, rolling up jelly-roll fashion, and slicing into small pinwheels. A brief baking made a delicious, not too sweet, melt-in-your mouth snack. My children now look forward to them when I bake at home.

If you do not have enough dough left for a full recipe of anything, wrap it tightly with food wrap, label, and freeze. It may be defrosted and mixed into additional leftover dough later.

BAKING

Baking times will be given under each individual recipe. Some general rules do apply throughout, however. Almost every pastry requires a very hot, preheated oven and a brief period of high heat to set the bottom crust. Heat is always lowered to moderate to complete the baking. Double-crust pies with uncooked fillings require the longest baking times and hottest ovens. Single crusts that are to be blind-baked (partially baked before filling) will require the least time and heat. Sweet pastry browns more quickly than unsweetened, and pastry made from crumbs or nuts requires lower heat and sets faster than any other.

For crusts that are to be baked either partially or completely before filling, you must keep the unfilled pastry from bubbling and collapsing. Try either of the following methods:

1. Weight the bottom crust with a pie plate of slightly smaller size (but same shape). Disposable aluminum tins work very well.

2. Line the bottom crust with parchment paper, foil, or brown paper. Cover with a substantial layer of rice, dried beans, or dried peas (which may be reused for this purpose) or with baking weights, which are made specifically for prebaking or partially baking (blind baking) unfilled bottom crusts.

FREEZING AND STORING PIE CRUSTS

Unfilled, unbaked pie shells may be frozen for up to 6 months. (If you make pastry in quantity you can freeze it and keep it.) Freeze shells separately, by placing wax paper between each frozen shell, and stack. Seal in freezer wrap or plastic bags and label. Unfilled, unbaked frozen shells do not need defrosting.

I have frozen almost all main-course and dessert pies, unbaked, with wonderful results. They may be kept up to 6 months without adverse effects. After preparing, freeze the unbaked pie immediately, by placing it in a plastic bag, and sealing it. Label with type and date. All frozen main-course pies can be baked *without* defrosting. Simply place in a preheated 500° oven and bake for 15 minutes. Then lower temperature to 375° and bake for approximately 45 minutes more.

Do not freeze cream, custard, or meringue pies. The cream and custard separate and get watery and the meringue toughens and shrinks.

I also do not recommend freezing baked pies—either main-course or dessert. Reheating them in a traditional oven will produce soggy pies. (I am told that some people do reheat frozen, baked pies in a microwave oven with good results. If you wish to do so, follow the directions that were included with your microwave oven.)

Chapter

CRUSTS
AND
TOPPINGS

Two

PASTRY CRUSTS

Before you start making pie crust, go over the general instructions until you are familiar with the basic procedures and feel comfortable with the steps required. Although the following recipes give instructions for hand mixing, use whatever method you prefer for combining the ingredients—by hand or with an electric mixer or food processor.

MOM'S FLAKY PASTRY

This is the most basic of all pastries and may be used for any recipe in this book. The other pastry recipes offer variety in texture and taste.

YIELD: Two 9-inch pie shells, or pastry for one 9-inch double-crust pie.

USE: All purpose.
May be frozen unbaked.

2 cups all-purpose flour
½ teaspoon salt
1 cup vegetable shortening (or lard)
¼ cup ice water, approximately

Mix flour and salt together in a bowl. Cut shortening into flour until mixture resembles coarse meal. Sprinkle with water, a tablespoon at a time, mixing quickly with a fork after each spoonful. Add only enough water so dough holds together and can be formed into a ball. Divide dough into two equal portions and form each into a smooth ball, handling as little as possible. Roll dough out onto lightly floured surface.

VARIATIONS

To alter the flavor of the pastry, add any one of the following along with the shortening:

¾ cup grated firm cheese (cheddar, Fontina, Gruyère)
2 teaspoons sesame seeds, poppy seeds, or caraway seeds
1 teaspoon grated orange or lemon peel
1 teaspoon celery seeds
1 teaspoon dried and chopped dill weed, chives, or parsley
1 teaspoon ground nutmeg or cinnamon
½ teaspoon curry powder

BASIC BUTTER PASTRY

This is a bit richer and less flaky than Mom's Flaky Pastry, but they may still be used interchangeably.

YIELD: Two 9-inch pie shells, or pastry for one 9-inch double-crust pie.

USE: All purpose.
May be frozen unbaked.

2 cups all-purpose flour
¼ teaspoon salt
¾ cup unsalted (sweet) butter, chilled
¼ cup ice water, approximately

Mix flour and salt together in a bowl. Cut butter into flour until mixture resembles coarse meal. Sprinkle with ice water, a tablespoon at a time, mixing quickly with a fork after each spoonful. Add only enough water so dough holds together and can be formed into a ball. Divide dough into two equal portions and form each into a smooth ball, handling as little as possible. Roll dough out onto lightly floured surface.

SWEET PASTRY

Because of the sugar content, this pastry browns more quickly than the more traditional pastries, so the oven temperature should be lowered slightly.

YIELD: Two 9-inch pie shells or pastry for one 9-inch double-crust pie.

USE: Fruit tarts, crumb-topped fruit pies, all dessert pies with patterned top crusts.
May be frozen unbaked.

- **2 cups all-purpose flour**
- **5 teaspoons superfine sugar**
- **1 egg, cold**
- **1 tablespoon ice water (flavored with vanilla, orange juice, or liquor, if desired)**
- **⅔ cup unsalted (sweet) butter, chilled**

Mix flour and sugar together in a bowl. Blend egg and liquid(s) together in a separate bowl. Cut butter into flour until mixture resembles coarse meal. Sprinkle with egg mixture, a tablespoon at a time, mixing quickly with a fork after each spoonful. Add only enough liquid so dough holds together and can be formed into a ball. Divide dough into two equal portions and form each into a smooth ball, handling as little as possible. Roll dough out onto lightly floured surface.

TART PASTRY

This produces a heavier crust and stands up well to fresh fruit; however, it is not flaky and does not make a good top crust.

YIELD: 10 to 12 tart shells or two 9-inch pie shells.

USE: All purpose.
May be frozen unbaked.

- **2 cups all-purpose flour**
- **2 tablespoons sugar**
- **¼ teaspoon salt**
- **1 hard-cooked egg yolk**
- **¾ cup unsalted (sweet) butter (or margarine), chilled**
- **¼ cup ice water, approximately**

Mix flour, sugar, and salt together in mixing bowl. Chop in egg yolk, then cut in butter. Sprinkle with water, a tablespoon at a time, mixing quickly with a fork after each spoonful. Add only enough water so dough holds together and can be formed into a ball. Roll out the dough as for pies but cut individual circles about 1 inch larger than the tart pan (most are about 3½ inches). Fit the circle into the tart pan, folding the excess dough evenly under the edge to make a ridge. Flute the edge with your fingers or crimp with the tines of a fork.

Note: If you don't have tart pans, you can make tart shells on inverted muffin tins or custard cups by fitting the pastry circles over the cups. (Bake in preheated 450°F oven for 10 minutes and cool before filling.) These can only be used to hold precooked filling or fresh fruit that does not need to be baked.

WHOLE WHEAT PASTRY

Whole wheat pastry is difficult to make, so you may want to master the other pastry recipes before working with this one.

YIELD: Two 9-inch pie shells or one 9-inch double-crust pie.

USE: All purpose.
May be frozen unbaked.

2½ cups whole wheat flour
    Dash of salt
1 tablespoon sugar (optional)
⅓ to ½ cup vegetable oil
6 tablespoons ice water, approximately

Mix flour, salt, and sugar (if desired) together in a bowl. Blend in oil, then ice water, mixing with a fork until it forms a ball. If pastry is too crumbly, you may want to add 1 beaten egg. Divide dough into two equal portions and form each into a ball, handling as little as possible. Roll dough out onto lightly floured surface.

Note: Lard, butter, or shortening may be used in place of the oil, but this makes the dough harder to work with. Decrease flour to 2 cups if you use a solid rather than a liquid fat.

CREAM CHEESE PASTRY

Another rich pastry that is especially nice with jam turnovers or fruit tarts.

YIELD: Two 9-inch pie shells or one 9-inch double-crust pie.

USE: All purpose.
May be frozen unbaked.

2 cups all-purpose flour
¼ teaspoon salt
1 cup unsalted (sweet) butter, chilled
1 cup cream cheese, chilled

Combine flour and salt in mixing bowl. Cut in the butter and cream cheese and form into a ball. Chill in plastic wrap at least 6 hours before rolling out on floured surface.

CRUMB CRUSTS

GRAHAM CRACKER CRUST

A crumb crust used unbaked must be thoroughly chilled (about 4 hours) before filling.

YIELD: One 9-inch pie shell.

USE: Cream, chiffon, or cheese pies.

BAKING TIME: Unfilled, 375°F for approximately 8 minutes.
May be frozen unbaked.

2 cups graham cracker crumbs
2 to 4 tablespoons sugar (depending on sweetness desired)
⅓ cup unsalted (sweet) butter (or margarine), melted
¼ teaspoon cinnamon, nutmeg, or ginger; or ½ teaspoon grated lemon or orange rind (optional)

Combine crumbs and sugar (and flavoring if desired) in medium mixing bowl. Pour melted butter over crumb mixture and blend with fingers until crumbs are well coated and begin to hold together. Butter only the bottom of a 9-inch pie plate. Drop graham mixture into prepared plate. Gently and evenly press the mixture over bottom and up sides of plate. Neatly finish off rim. Bake as directed above or until edge is just a bit brown. Cool before filling.

COOKIE CRUMB CRUST

YIELD: One 9-inch pie shell.

USE: Cream, chiffon, or cheese pies.

BAKING TIME: Unfilled, 375°F for approximately 8 minutes. May be frozen unbaked.

2 cups finely ground cookie crumbs (chocolate, vanilla, or lemon wafers or gingersnaps)
½ cup unsalted (sweet) butter (or margarine), melted

Place crumbs in medium mixing bowl. Pour melted butter over mixture and blend with your fingers until crumbs are well coated and begin to hold together. Butter the bottom only of a 9-inch pie plate. Drop the cookie mixture into the prepared plate and gently and evenly press mixture over bottom and up sides of plate. Neatly finish off rim. Bake as directed above or until edge is just a bit brown. Cool before filling.

NUT CRUST

Make sure the nuts are finely ground so the dough holds together while it is being rolled out.

YIELD: One 9-inch pie shell.

USE: Any pie with cooked filling (cannot withstand long baking).

BAKING TIME: 375°F for 18 to 20 minutes. May be frozen unbaked.

¾ cup all-purpose flour
½ cup finely ground walnuts, almonds, pecans, peanuts, or hazelnuts
2 teaspoons sugar
¼ teaspoon unsalted (sweet) butter, well chilled
1 egg yolk, beaten
1 teaspoon ice water, if needed

Combine flour, nuts, and sugar in medium mixing bowl. Cut in butter until mixture resembles coarse meal. Mix in egg yolk. If necessary, add ice water until pastry begins to hold together. Form pastry into a ball and wrap with food wrap or aluminum foil. Refrigerate for at least 1 hour or until thoroughly chilled. Roll out as you would any other pastry (see page 16). Butter the bottom only of a 9-inch pie plate and lay pastry in it. Trim dough neatly around the edge of plate. Do not crimp. Prick bottom with the tines of a fork and bake as directed above or until lightly browned. Cool before filling.

TOPPINGS

Meringue adds so much to a cream pie and it is easy to make when you follow a few simple rules:

1. Be sure the sugar is thoroughly incorporated into the beaten egg whites; otherwise, the undissolved sugar will cause brown, syrupy beads to form on the surface of the baked meringue. (Using superfine sugar is a big help.)

2. Be careful not to overwhip the meringue, making it dry rather than stiff and shiny, for this will cause it to crack when baking.

3. Make sure the pie filling is set before topping it with meringue.

4. Be certain that the entire surface of the pie is covered and sealed with meringue. If not, it will shrink and the filling will leak.

5. Do not overbake a meringue-topped pie. It should never take more than 12 minutes.

6. Cool the pie in a draft-free place for at least 30 minutes before cutting. The slightest breeze will cause the meringue to shrink and fall.

Whipped cream and sour cream toppings can be used interchangeably. Their use depends on your taste. Whipped cream is particularly good on cream pies and sour cream works well with fresh fruit. Either makes a pretty dessert.

WHIPPED CREAM TOPPING

If you wish to use whipped cream in a pastry tube for decorating, or if you want to hold a topped pie for later use, add ½ teaspoon unflavored gelatin dissolved in 1 tablespoon water for each cup of cream. Heat the gelatin/water until gelatin is totally dissolved; then cool, stirring constantly. Add to cream after you have started beating it and just as it begins to thicken. This will give you an extrafirm whipped cream topping.

YIELD: Topping for one 9-inch pie.

USE: Topping for cream, custard, or fruit pies. Do not bake. May be frozen.

1 **cup very cold heavy cream**
2 **tablespoons confectioners' or superfine sugar**
Pinch of cream of tartar

Place a bowl and beater in freezer until well chilled. Remove from freezer, pour very cold cream into the bowl, and begin beating at once. As cream begins to thicken, add sugar and cream of tartar. Continue beating at high speed until cream is stiff and holds a peak. Do not overbeat. Immediately spread on top of chilled, filled pie. You may wish to use a fork or icing comb to create a pattern on top of the pie. You can also decorate the top with sprinkles, grated chocolate, grated peel, candied flowers, or other decorative edible foods appropriate to the flavor of the pie. Refrigerate until ready to serve.

VARIATIONS

Any of the following flavors may be added with the sugar to each cup of cream:

1 **to 2 tablespoons unsweetened cocoa**
1 **teaspoon vanilla**
2 **teaspoons liquor**
¼ **teaspoon ginger or cinnamon**
1 **teaspoon fine instant coffee powder (not the large, freeze-dried granules)**
1 **tablespoon finely grated orange, lemon, or lime rind**
¼ **teaspoon almond extract**

Or in place of sugar use:

¼ **cup maple syrup**
3 **tablespoons brown sugar**
1 **tablespoon honey**

SOUR CREAM TOPPING

Any of the suggested flavoring variations for Whipped Cream Topping may be used, in the same proportions.

YIELD: Topping for one 9-inch pie.

USE: Topping for cream or fruit pies. Do not bake. May be frozen.

1½ **cups dairy sour cream**
2 **tablespoons superfine sugar**

Whip sugar into sour cream until dissolved. Refrigerate for at least 30 minutes. Spread on top of chilled, filled pie. Refrigerate until ready to serve.

AUNT FRANCES' NEVER-FAIL MERINGUE

After covering a pie with this topping, you can make it even more attractive by lifting the meringue with the back of a spoon into soft peaks.

PREHEAT OVEN: 400°F.

YIELD: Topping for one 9-inch pie.

USE: Topping for cream or fruit pies.

BAKING TIME: 10 minutes or until meringue is golden.

½ **cup water**
1 **tablespoon cornstarch dissolved in 1 tablespoon water**
3 **egg whites**
6 **tablespoons superfine sugar**

In small saucepan bring the ½ cup water to a boil. Add the cornstarch solution and cook, stirring constantly, until water is clear. Remove from heat and cool. With electric mixer on low, begin to beat the egg whites in a large bowl. Increase speed and alternately add the cooled liquid and the sugar to the egg whites, beating until stiff and shiny. Place a large amount of meringue on top of the center of a filled baked pie shell. Put small spoonfuls of meringue around the edge of shell. Spread from the center out to meet the edge, being sure that the entire top is covered and edges are sealed. Bake as directed above and cool gradually, away from drafts.

Chapter

MAIN-COURSE PIES
AND
APPETIZERS

Three

CHICKEN

CHICKEN-IN-EVERY-POTPIE

It is only fitting that the recipes should begin with everyone's all-time favorite main-course pie. A kitchen staple for generations with nothing to compare to its goodness and flavor.

PREHEAT OVEN: 500°F.
PASTRY NEEDED: Unbaked 9-inch double-crust pie.
BAKING TIME: 15 minutes at 500°F, 20 minutes at 375°F.
SERVINGS: 4 to 6.
May be frozen unbaked.

- 4 to 5 pound chicken, cut up*
  Salt and pepper to taste
- 4 carrots, sliced
- 3 medium-size potatoes, diced
- 1 medium-size onion, diced
- ¾ cup frozen petit peas
- 2 tablespoons butter or chicken fat
- 1 tablespoon flour

Place cut-up chicken in heavy pot, cover with water, add salt and pepper, and bring to a boil. Reduce heat and simmer, covered, until chicken is

Chicken-In-Every-Potpie prepared with Mom's Flaky Pastry and decorated with chicken cut-outs. Hearty and delicious.

done, about an hour. Remove chicken from broth to cool. Strain and reserve broth. When chicken is cool, remove skin and bones and discard. Pull or cut meat into large chunks. Place in large mixing bowl and set aside.

Pour 3 cups of reserved chicken broth in saucepan. Bring to boil and add carrots, potatoes, and onion. Simmer gently until vegetables are just barely cooked. Remove from heat and add frozen peas and salt and pepper to taste.

Melt the butter in a small saucepan over very low heat. Mix in the flour and stir until completely blended. Remove from heat.

Strain vegetables, reserving broth. Stir 2 cups of this hot, seasoned cooking broth into butter-flour mixture. Mix well with a wire whisk until you have a well-blended sauce. Add to chicken meat in mixing bowl, gently mix in vegetables, and add additional broth if mixture is too thick. Put chicken mixture into pie shell and add additional stock if more liquid is needed to fill the crust. Cap and finish as described on pages 17-18. Bake as directed above or until golden.

* This can also be made with 2 pounds boned and skinned chicken breasts. Cube the meat and cook over medium heat along with the vegetables in 2 cups canned broth and enough water to cover. This should take about 20 minutes. Season to taste, prepare the sauce, and proceed as directed above.

LAYERED CHICKEN PIE

Perhaps the quickest of all chicken pies, this is wonderful as a main course or an appetizer. Serve with a tossed green salad or a vegetable vinaigrette. It's a very easy surprise-guest meal.

PREHEAT OVEN: 500°F.
PASTRY NEEDED: Unbaked 9-inch double-crust pie.
BAKING TIME: 15 minutes at 500°F, 20 minutes at 375°F.
SERVINGS: 8 to 10 as an appetizer; 4 to 6 as a main course.
May be frozen unbaked.

- 4 cups diced cooked chicken
- 1 to 1½ cups chicken stock
- 2 cups grated Gruyère cheese
- 6 slices Virginia ham

Place chicken in a large mixing bowl and slowly add stock until chicken is quite moist but not wet. Place 2 cups diced chicken in the bottom of pie shell. Sprinkle with 1 cup cheese and add ham slices and the remaining cheese. Top with the remaining 2 cups chicken, cap, and finish as described on pages 17-18. Brush with egg wash (see page 18), and bake as directed above or until golden.

ITALIAN CHICKEN PIE

A tasty variation, rather like a chicken cacciatore encased in pastry. A wonderful meal with a tossed green salad, bread sticks, and a light Italian wine.

PREHEAT OVEN: 500°F.
PASTRY NEEDED: Unbaked 9-inch double-crust pie.
BAKING TIME: 15 minutes at 500°F, 20 minutes at 375°F.
SERVINGS: 4 to 6.
May be frozen unbaked.

2 pounds chicken breasts and thighs, boned, skinned, and cubed
5 carrots, sliced
1 large green pepper, diced
4 stalks celery, diced
1 large onion, diced
2 cloves garlic, minced
2 cups chopped and seeded Italian tomatoes, or 2 cups canned crushed tomatoes
1 cup chicken stock
1 teaspoon basil
¼ teaspoon oregano
1 bay leaf
   Salt and pepper to taste
2 tablespoons butter or margarine
1½ tablespoons flour

Place all ingredients, except butter and flour, in a heavy pot. Add water to cover, if necessary. Bring to a boil, reduce heat, and simmer, covered, for about 40 minutes or until flavors have begun to blend. Remove bay leaf.

Melt the butter in a small saucepan over low heat. Mix in the flour and stir until completely blended. Remove from heat. Whisk approximately 1 cup of cooking liquid into the flour/butter mixture. Stir until mixed well, then add to the chicken and vegetables. Gently mix all together and pour into pie shell. Cap and finish as described on pages 17-18. Bake as directed above or until golden.

CHICKEN CURRY PIE

Eastern spices add zest and interest to this chicken pie. Serve with a homemade chutney, cucumber and yogurt salad, and white wine, beer, or iced tea. Fresh fruit for dessert completes the menu.

PREHEAT OVEN: 500°F.
PASTRY NEEDED: Unbaked 9-inch double-crust pie.
BAKING TIME: 15 minutes at 500°F, 20 minutes at 375°F.
SERVINGS: 4 to 6.
May be frozen unbaked.

2 pounds chicken breasts and thighs, boned, skinned, and cubed
1 cup cooked chick peas
1 large green pepper, diced
½ cup applesauce
1 cup chicken stock
3 tablespoons curry powder
¼ teaspoon cumin
¼ teaspoon grated orange rind
   Salt and pepper to taste
1 large onion, diced
4 carrots, sliced
¾ cup raisins
2 cups chopped and seeded Italian tomatoes, or 2 cups canned crushed tomatoes
¼ teaspoon cinnamon
2 tablespoons butter or margarine
1½ tablespoons flour

Place all ingredients except butter and flour in heavy pot and add water to cover, if necessary. Bring to a boil, reduce heat, and simmer, covered, for about 40 minutes, or until flavors have begun to blend. Melt the butter in a small saucepan over very low heat. Mix in the flour and stir until completely blended. Remove from heat. Whisk about 1 cup of the curry sauce into the flour/butter mixture. Stir until well mixed. Add to the chicken and vegetables and gently stir all together. Pour into pie shell, cap, and finish as described on pages 17-18. Bake as directed above or until golden.

CHICKEN OYSTER PIE

A great way to use leftover chicken and to stretch a small supply of fresh oysters. You can use less chicken if you have the oysters to spare.

PREHEAT OVEN: 500°F.

PASTRY NEEDED: Unbaked 9-inch double-crust pie.

BAKING TIME: 15 minutes at 500°F, 20 minutes at 375°F.

SERVINGS: 4 to 6.
May be frozen unbaked.

> 2 cups cooked chicken, diced
> 2 cups fresh oysters, drained (reserve liquid)
> 2 cups chicken stock, approximately
> 3 tablespoons butter
> 1 small onion, diced
> 3 stalks celery, minced
> ¼ teaspoon dill
> 3 to 5 drops Tabasco
> 3 tablespoons flour
> Salt and pepper to taste
> 1½ cups frozen petit peas

Mix the cooked chicken and oysters together. Place in bottom of pie shell. Combine reserved oyster liquid with enough chicken stock to make at least 2½ cups. Set aside. Melt the butter in a heavy saucepan over medium heat, add the onion, celery, and dill, and cook slowly over low heat until onion and celery are limp and have begun to lose their liquid. Add the Tabasco and stir in flour. When well blended add oyster liquid/chicken stock combination. Cook over medium heat, stirring constantly, until mixture comes to a boil. Lower heat and cook for about 5 minutes. Remove from heat. Stir in salt and pepper and peas and pour sauce over the chicken/oyster mixture. Cap and finish as described on pages 17-18. Bake as directed above or until golden.

BRUNSWICK CHICKEN PIE

This makes a wonderful hearty winter meal using corn, tomatoes, lima beans, and okra found in your freezer, harvested from the bounty of summer.

PREHEAT OVEN: 500°F.

PASTRY NEEDED: Unbaked 9-inch double-crust pie.

BAKING TIME: 15 minutes at 500°F, 20 minutes at 375°F.

SERVINGS: 4 to 6.
May be frozen unbaked.

4 to 5 pound chicken, cut up
½ teaspoon thyme
¼ teaspoon margarine
  Salt and pepper to taste
1 cup whole-kernel corn
1 large onion, diced
1½ cups peeled, seeded, and cubed tomatoes
1 cup lima beans
1 cup diced okra
¼ pound slab bacon, diced
2 tablespoons butter
3 tablespoons flour

Place chicken in heavy saucepan. Add thyme, margarine, and salt and pepper to taste. Cover with water, bring to a boil, reduce heat, and simmer, covered, until chicken is done, about 1 hour. Remove chicken from broth to cool. Strain and reserve broth.

When chicken is cooled, remove skin and bones from meat and discard. Cut chicken meat into large pieces and place in a mixing bowl. Put vegetables and bacon in a large, heavy pot and cover with the reserved chicken broth. Bring to boil, lower heat, and simmer gently until vegetables are just barely cooked. Remove from heat and strain, reserving broth.

Melt the butter in a small saucepan over very low heat. Mix in the flour and stir until completely blended. Remove from heat and stir in 2 cups of the broth used to cook the vegetables and chicken. Whisk until well blended and a creamy sauce has been achieved. You may have to cook over low heat for a few minutes. Mix the chicken, vegetables, and sauce together. Pour into pie shell, cap, and finish as described on pages 17-18. Bake as directed above or until golden.

Brunswick Chicken Pie baked in Mom's Flaky Pastry with a cutout top.

CHICKEN AND LEEK PIE

Based on a traditional Spanish recipe, this can also be made with onions in place of leeks, but the taste will not be quite as delicate.

PREHEAT OVEN: 500°F.

PASTRY NEEDED: Unbaked 9-inch double-crust pie.

BAKING TIME: 15 minutes at 500°F, 20 minutes at 375°F.

SERVINGS: 4 to 6.
May be frozen unbaked.

½ pound pork breakfast sausage
3 pounds boneless chicken breasts, cubed
3 pounds leeks, washed, trimmed, and sliced
2 cloves garlic, minced
3 tablespoons minced fresh parsley
¼ teaspoon sage
2 tablespoons butter
3 tablespoons flour
1 cup heavy cream
1 cup chicken broth

Place sausage in large, heavy skillet over medium heat. As it begins to cook, add the cubed chicken and leeks. Add the garlic, parsley, and sage. Watch carefully, stirring frequently until the meat has cooked and the leeks are well wilted. Remove from heat. In another skillet melt butter over medium heat. Stir in flour and cook until flour and butter are well blended. Stir in cream and broth. Cook over medium heat until medium white sauce has been formed. Add the chicken and sausage mixture to the sauce and stir to blend well; add additional cream or stock to thin down if necessary. Pour mixture into pie shell, cap, and finish as described on pages 17-18. Bake as directed above or until golden.

COCKALEEKIE PIE

Ham and chicken make a very sophisticated taste combination in this recipe, based on an old favorite from the British Isles. You might want to reserve some of the broth from the chicken and make a gravy to pour over this pie when serving.

PREHEAT OVEN: 500°F.

PASTRY NEEDED: Unbaked 9-inch double-crust pie.

BAKING TIME: 15 minutes at 500°F, 20 minutes at 375°F.

SERVINGS: 4 to 6.
May be frozen unbaked.

4 to 5 pound chicken, cut up
1 medium onion, diced
1 carrot, sliced
2 stalks celery, sliced
2 tablespoons minced fresh parsley
1 bay leaf
1 pound Virginia ham, diced
4 tablespoons butter
6 leeks, washed, trimmed, and chopped
¼ pound fresh mushrooms, chopped
3 tablespoons flour
2 tablespoons sherry

Place chicken and next 5 ingredients in a large pot. Cover with water, bring to boil over high heat, reduce heat to low, and simmer gently, covered, for about 1 hour or until chicken is tender. Remove from heat. Remove chicken from broth and strain broth into a large saucepan. Discard vegetables and herbs but reserve broth. When chicken is cool, remove meat from bones in large pieces. Discard bones and skin. Place chicken meat and ham in mixing bowl and set aside.

Melt butter in a large skillet over medium heat. Add leeks and mushrooms and sauté until tender. Stir in flour and mix until well blended. Add sherry and 2½ cups of the reserved chicken broth. Whisk gently until a light cream sauce has formed. Toss with the chicken and ham and pour into pie shell. Cap and finish as described on pages 17-18. Bake as directed above or until golden.

PÂTÉ PIE

Not really pâté, but it is similar. Serve as an appetizer with pickled vegetables and mustard or as a main course with green vegetables vinaigrette, followed by a light dessert.

PREHEAT OVEN: 500°F.

PASTRY NEEDED: Unbaked 9-inch double-crust pie.

BAKING TIME: 15 minutes at 500°F, 20 minutes at 375°F.

SERVINGS: 12 as an appetizer; 4 to 6 as a main course.
May be frozen unbaked.

¼ **pound butter**
2 **tablespoons vegetable oil**
2 **pound chicken livers**
1 **cup chopped onion**
¼ **teaspoon tarragon**
   Salt and pepper to taste
1 **cup red wine**
½ **cup chicken broth**
1 **tablespoon brandy**
2 **cups whole small mushrooms**
   Roux of 3 tablespoons flour and 2 tablespoons butter, if necessary

Melt the butter and vegetable oil over medium heat in heavy casserole. Add the chicken livers and cook, stirring frequently, until livers begin to set and brown. Add the onion, tarragon, and salt and pepper. Cook, stirring frequently, until onion begins to wilt. Add the wine and chicken broth and cover. Cook over medium heat for about 30 minutes or until chicken livers are well cooked. Remove from heat. Stir in the brandy and mushrooms. If not thick enough, make a roux and whisk gently into the chicken liver mixture. Pour into pie shell, cap, and finish as described on pages 17-18. Bake as directed above or until golden.

TURKEY

TURKEY POTPIE

Turkey potpie has traditionally been made with the remains of a large holiday bird. However, turkey breasts, legs, and wings are now available all year long and can be prepared especially for pie. If you plan to use leftover meat, you will need at least 2 cups of leftover gravy. Whichever method is used, turkey potpie is a great way to enjoy the all-American bird.

PREHEAT OVEN: 500°F.

PASTRY NEEDED: Unbaked 9-inch double-crust pie.

BAKING TIME: 15 minutes at 500°F, 30 minutes at 375°F.

SERVINGS: 4 to 6.
May be frozen unbaked.

3 cubed cubed cooked turkey meat
4 carrots, sliced
1 medium onion, diced
2 cups leftover gravy (or 2½ cups turkey broth, 2 tablespoons butter, and 3 tablespoons flour*)
3 medium potatoes, diced
4 stalks celery, peeled and sliced
Salt and pepper to taste

Place all ingredients in a mixing bowl, stir to mix, and turn into pie shell. Cap and finish as described on pages 17-18. Bake as directed above or until golden.

*If you are using turkey broth, melt butter in heavy frying pan. Blend in flour, stir until well blended, add turkey broth, and cook over medium heat for about 5 minutes or until a nice sauce has been formed. Add all other ingredients and proceed as above.

LEFTOVER-TURKEY PIE

A special way to use up leftover holiday turkey. This pie also makes a great first course for a fancy dinner party. If you freeze leftover meat you can cook this up for surprise guests at a moment's notice. Serve with a light soup and a tossed green salad and you have a gourmet meal.

PREHEAT OVEN: 500°F.

PASTRY NEEDED: Unbaked 9-inch double-crust pie.

BAKING TIME: 10 minutes at 500°F, 20 minutes at 350°F.

SERVINGS: 4 to 6.
May be frozen unbaked.

½ pound bacon
½ cup minced onion
¼ cup minced celery
1 large apple, peeled, cored, and diced
¼ cup chopped nuts
3 tablespoons butter
3 tablespoons flour
1¾ cups chicken stock
¼ cup dry white wine
Nutmeg to taste
Salt and pepper to taste
2½ cups finely chopped cooked turkey
¾ cup grated Parmesan (or Romano) cheese

Place bacon in heavy frying pan and fry until crisp. Drain off all but 2 tablespoons bacon fat. Add the onion, celery, apple, and nuts. Cook over very low heat until vegetables are wilted. Remove from heat and set aside. Melt butter in large saucepan, stir in flour, and mix until well blended. Add the chicken stock and wine and cook until a light cream sauce has been formed. Add nutmeg, salt and pepper, cooked vegetables, and turkey. Stir until well blended and remove from heat. Sprinkle ¼ cup grated cheese on bottom of shell and cover with half the turkey mixture. Sprinkle ¼ cup grated cheese on bottom of pie shell and cover with other half of turkey mixture. Top with remaining ¼ cup grated cheese, finish with a lattice top, brush with egg wash (see page 18), and bake as directed above or until golden brown.

HUNTER'S PIE

One of my favorite hearty meals. The flavors meld beautifully. I usually make it with fresh turkey so I can have some turkey stock, but it is just as good using leftover turkey.

PREHEAT OVEN: 500°F.

PASTRY NEEDED: Unbaked 9-inch double-crust pie.

BAKING TIME: 15 minutes at 500°F, 20 minutes at 375°F.

SERVINGS: 4 to 6.
May be frozen unbaked.

1 **pound sweet Italian sausage, sliced**
1 **clove garlic, minced**
2 **tablespoons tomato paste**
1 **medium-size potato, sliced**
½ **teaspoon thyme**
  Salt and pepper to taste
1 **medium-size onion, diced**
2 **cups canned plum tomatoes, with juice**
3 **carrots, sliced**
¼ **cup diced green pepper**
¼ **teaspoon sage**
2 **cups cubed cooked turkey meat**

Place sausage in large, heavy saucepan over medium heat. Cook, stirring constantly, until fat is rendered and sausage begins to lose its raw color. If you have a lot of fat, drain off all but about 2 tablespoons. Add all other ingredients except turkey and cook over medium heat for about 20 minutes. Remove from heat, add turkey, stir to mix, and pour into pie shell. Cap and finish as described on pages 17-18. Bake as directed above or until golden.

GROUND TURKEY PIE

Fresh ground turkey is a great alternative to ground beef. It is very low in fat and a welcome way to cut calories.

PREHEAT OVEN: 500°F.

PASTRY NEEDED: Unbaked 9-inch double-crust pie.

BAKING TIME: 15 minutes at 500°F, 20 minutes at 375°F.

SERVINGS: 4 to 6 as a main course. May be frozen unbaked.

2 **pounds fresh ground turkey**
1 **teaspoon thyme**
1 **cup cooked chopped spinach, well drained**
2 **drops Tabasco**
1 **large onion, grated**
¼ **teaspoon sage**
1½ **cups mashed cooked potatoes**
   Salt and pepper to taste

Combine all ingredients in large mixing bowl. Turn into pie shell, cap, and finish as described on pages 17-18. Bake as directed above or until golden.

BEEF

SHEPHERD'S PIE

Although I generally use veal, any other type of ground meat will work well in this recipe, which is based on the traditional English leftover-meat pie.

PREHEAT OVEN: 500°F.

PASTRY NEEDED: Unbaked 9-inch double-crust pie.

BAKING TIME: 15 minutes at 500°F, 35 to 45 minutes at 375°F.

SERVINGS: 4 to 6. May be frozen unbaked.

¼ **pound butter**
2 **tablespoons vegetable oil**
2 **pounds ground beef (or veal, lamb, pork, poultry, etc.)**
1 **large onion, grated**
1 **teaspoon thyme**
½ **teaspoon dill**
1 **cup cooked chopped spinach, thoroughly drained**
3 **to 4 cups mashed potatoes**
   Salt and pepper to taste
1 **tablespoon melted butter**
1 **tablespoon bread crumbs**

Melt the ¼ pound butter and vegetable oil in heavy saucepan over medium heat. Add the veal, onion, and herbs and cook, stirring constantly, until meat begins to lose its color. Add the spinach and 1 cup mashed potatoes. Stir to blend and add salt and pepper to taste. Place mixture in pie shell and use remaining mashed potatoes to make a top crust, mounding slightly in the center. Brush with 1 tablespoon melted butter, sprinkle with bread crumbs, and bake as directed above or until golden.

Savory Shepherd's Pie made with Mom's Flaky Pastry and sprinkled with bread crumbs. Real comfort food on a cold winter's night.

OLD-FASHIONED BEEF PIE

When I was a child, my mother made beef pies from leftover roasts. But since I never seem to have leftover roast beef, I just use stewing beef and from time to time have even used leftover beef stew to make a pie.

PREHEAT OVEN: 500°F.

PASTRY NEEDED: Unbaked 9-inch double-crust pie.

BAKING TIME: 15 minutes at 500°F, 20 minutes at 375°F.

SERVINGS: 4 to 6.
May be frozen unbaked.

- 2 **pounds lean stewing beef, cubed**
- ¼ **cup flour**
- 3 **tablespoons butter**
- 2 **tablespoons margarine**
- 1 **cup beef stock**
- 5 **carrots, sliced**
- 1 **large onion, diced**
- 3 **potatoes, cubed**
  Salt and pepper to taste
- 1 **cup frozen petit peas**

Dredge stewing beef in flour. Melt butter and margarine together in a large, heavy Dutch oven, add meat, and brown on all sides. Cover with the beef stock and cook, covered, over medium heat for 45 minutes or until beef is beginning to get tender. Add water if additional liquid is needed. Stir in vegetables, except for peas, and cook about 10 minutes. Add salt and pepper to taste, remove from heat, and stir in peas. Pour into pie shell, cap, and finish as described on pages 17-18. Bake as directed above or until golden.

HIGH THYME PIE

The flavors of thyme and sage are predominant in this pie. It is a great first course served with a horseradish sauce; as a main course it can be eaten either hot or cold.

PREHEAT OVEN: 500°F.

PASTRY NEEDED: Unbaked 9-inch double-crust pie.

BAKING TIME: 15 minutes at 500°F, 35 to 40 minutes at 350°F.

SERVINGS: 4 to 6.
May be frozen unbaked.

- 2 **pounds lean ground beef**
- 1 **large onion, minced**
- 1½ **cups cooked chopped spinach, well drained**
- ¼ **teaspoon sage**
  Salt and pepper to taste
- 3 **cups prepared poultry stuffing cubes**
- 2 **tablespoons minced fresh parsley**
- 1 **teaspoon thyme**
- ¼ **teaspoon orange zest**

Place all ingredients in a medium-size bowl and mix with hands or wooden spoon until well blended. Place in shell, cap, and finish as described on pages 17-18. Bake as directed above or until golden.

BURGUNDY BEEF PIE

Based on the traditional French boeuf bourguignon, *this is a great party meal. Double the recipe and prepare it in pastry-lined lasagne-type pans for a buffet.*

PREHEAT OVEN: 500°F.

PASTRY NEEDED: Unbaked 9-inch double-crust pie.

BAKING TIME: 15 minutes at 500°F, 20 minutes at 375°F.

SERVINGS: 4 to 6.
May be frozen unbaked.

  2 **pounds lean stewing beef, cubed**
  2 **tablespoons flour**
    Salt and pepper to taste
  2 **tablespoons butter**
  1 **tablespoon vegetable oil**
  1 **medium-size onion, grated**
1½ **cups red wine**
1½ **cups beef broth**
 10 **small whole pearl onions**
  1 **clove garlic, crushed**
  1 **tablespoon tomato paste**
  ¼ **teaspoon rosemary**
 10 **small whole mushrooms**

Dredge cubed beef with flour and season lightly with salt and pepper. Melt butter and oil in large skillet over moderate heat. When melted, add grated onion and beef, sautéing meat on all sides. If necessary, add additional fat to keep meat from sticking. When beef has browned, pour off excess fat, add ½ cup red wine and ½ cup beef broth, and stir, scraping up any particles stuck to bottom of pan. Transfer meat and sauce to heavy casserole with lid. Add remaining red wine and beef broth, pearl onions, garlic, tomato paste, rosemary, and salt and pepper to taste. Cook, covered, over medium heat for about 1 hour or until meat is tender. Stir in mushrooms, pour into pie shell, cap, and finish as described on pages 17-18. Bake as directed above or until golden.

CUBAÑA PIE

Cubaña is based on a Latin American dish called picadillo, *in which raisins and olives are combined with meat to create a sweet/sour taste.*
It is an excellent buffet or party dish served with sour cream and chopped onions. Eat it hot or at room temperature.

PREHEAT OVEN: 500°F.

PASTRY NEEDED: Unbaked 9-inch double-crust pie.

BAKING TIME: 15 minutes at 500°F, 35 to 45 minutes at 350°F.

SERVINGS: 4 to 6.
May be frozen unbaked.

  1 **cup cooked white rice**
  1 **medium onion, grated**
  ¼ **cup dark raisins**
  1 **teaspoon chili powder**
  2 **to 3 drops Tabasco**
1½ **pounds ground beef**
  1 **clove garlic, crushed**
  2- **ounce jar of pimiento-stuffed olives with juice**
  ¾ **cup crushed tomatoes with juice**
  ⅛ **teaspoon black pepper**

Place all ingredients in medium-size bowl and blend thoroughly. Place mixture in pie shell, cap, and finish as described on pages 17-18. Bake as directed above or until golden.

STEAK AND KIDNEY PIE

Synonymous with the British Isles, steak and kidney pie is rarely served in the United States. For some, kidneys are an acquired taste; for others, something that will remain forever untried. For the former, you will be serving a favorite meal; for the latter you will have to sneak it in under an assumed name.

PREHEAT OVEN: 500°F.

PASTRY NEEDED: Unbaked 9-inch double-crust pie.

BAKING TIME: 15 minutes at 500°F, 20 minutes at 375°F.

SERVINGS: 4 to 6.
May be frozen unbaked.

2 **pounds beef kidneys**
2 **pounds sirloin, cubed**
3 **tablespoons flour**
6 **tablespoons butter**
2 **medium-size onions, diced**
1 **teaspoon rosemary**
   Salt and pepper to taste
2 **cups beef stock**
2 **tablespoons white wine**
¼ **pound mushrooms, sliced**

Place the beef kidneys in a large bowl, cover with water, and soak for about 1 hour. Drain, rinse, and cut into cubes, removing tubes and fat as you go. Set aside. Dredge sirloin cubes with flour. Melt butter and margarine in large, heavy saucepan, add the sirloin, and stir, browning on all sides. Add kidneys and onions and stir constantly, scraping up particles from bottom of pan. Add rosemary and salt and pepper to taste and cover with beef stock and white wine. Cook, covered, over medium heat for about 45 minutes or until you have a nice stew. Remove from heat. Stir in the sliced mushrooms, pour into pie shell, cap, and finish as described on pages 17-18. Bake as directed above or until golden.

CHILI CON CARNE PIE

Another version of chili in a pie. Accompany with sour cream, salsa, and grated cheese.

PREHEAT OVEN: 500°F.

PASTRY NEEDED: Unbaked 9-inch double-crust pie.

BAKING TIME: 15 minutes at 500°F, 35 to 45 minutes at 350°F.

SERVINGS: 4 to 6.
May be frozen unbaked.

1½ **pounds ground beef, lean**
½ **cup tomato paste**
2 **cloves garlic, minced**
2 **tablespoons chili powder**
   Dash Tabasco
1 **cup chopped and seeded tomatoes**
1 **whole onion**
¼ **cup seeded and chopped green chilis (optional)**
½ **teaspoon cumin**
   Salt and pepper to taste
1 **cup cooked pinto beans**

Place all ingredients except beans in medium-size bowl and stir thoroughly to blend. Gently mix in the cooked beans, pour into pie shell, cap, and finish as described on pages 17-18. Bake as directed above or until golden.

Chile Con Carne Pie baked in Mom's Flaky Pastry. The top was made with cactus cutouts and triangular-edged scalloping.

STEFADO PIE

*A tasty variation of a traditional Greek
family stew. I brush the top with
egg wash and sprinkle with sesame seeds.
Serve with a feta cheese salad
and a hearty beverage.*

PREHEAT OVEN: 500°F.

PASTRY NEEDED: Unbaked 9-inch
double-crust pie.

BAKING TIME: 15 minutes at 500°F,
20 minutes at 375°F.

SERVINGS: 4 to 6.
May be frozen unbaked.

2½ **pounds lean stewing beef,
cubed**
 3 **tablespoons flour**
   Salt and pepper to taste
 ¼ **pound butter**
 1 **tablespoon vegetable oil**
 ½ **cup peeled, seeded, and
chopped tomatoes**
 1 **cup tomato paste**
 ¼ **cup wine vinegar**
 ½ **cup red wine**
 2 **tablespoons dark brown sugar**
   **Tie in cheesecloth bag: 2 bay
leaves, 8 whole cloves, 1
cinnamon stick, 1 tablespoon
chopped fresh parsley, and 2
garlic cloves, cut in half**
 2 **pounds pearl onions, peeled
and cooked (or an equal
amount of canned or frozen,
thawed and drained.**

Dredge the stewing beef in flour and
salt and pepper. Melt the butter and
vegetable oil in a large, heavy saucepan
and add the stewing beef, stirring until well browned. Remove from heat.
Stir in the tomatoes, tomato paste,
vinegar, wine, and brown sugar. Add
the cheesecloth bag with spices and
herbs and cook, covered, over medium
heat for about 1 hour or until meat is
done. Remove from heat, discard spice
bag, add pearl onions, and stir until
mixed. Pour into pie shell, cap, and
finish as described on pages 17-18.
Bake as directed above or until
golden.

BEAN BAG PIE

*Lots of beans stretch a little bit of meat,
and to stretch your food budget even further,
you can eliminate the meat altogether
and have a vegetarian pie.
Either way, serve with sour cream,
salsa, and chopped fresh onion
and tomato. A great winter's meal.*

PREHEAT OVEN: 500°F.

PASTRY NEEDED: Unbaked 9-inch
cheddar cheese pie shell
(see Mom's Flaky Pastry variations,
page 22).

BAKING TIME: 15 minutes at 500°F,
20 minutes at 375°F.

SERVINGS: 4 to 6.
May be frozen unbaked.

 4 **cups cooked pinto beans**
 ¼ **pound lean ground beef**
 1 **tablespoon chopped fresh
coriander**
 ½ **teaspoon cumin**
   Salt and pepper to taste
 1 **cup cooked rice**
 ½ **cup tomato paste**
 3 **tablespoons chili powder**
 ¼ **teaspoon oregano**

Place all ingredients in a medium-size
bowl and stir to blend. Transfer to pie
shell, cap, and finish as described on
pages 17-18. Bake as directed above or
until golden.

GREEK MEAT PIE

Authentically made with filo dough, but easily adapted to pie pastry. Traditional Greek flavors make this a great party dish. Serve hot or cold.

PREHEAT OVEN: 500°F.

PASTRY NEEDED: Unbaked 9-inch double-crust pie.

BAKING TIME: 15 minutes at 500°F, 35 to 45 minutes at 350°F.

SERVINGS: 4 to 6.
May be frozen unbaked.

- 4 tablespoons olive oil
- 1 cup chopped onion
- ½ cup chopped fresh parsley
- ½ cup chopped walnuts
- 2 pounds very lean ground beef
- ½ teaspoon ground cumin
- ¼ teaspoon ground cinnamon
- ½ teaspoon chopped dried mint
- 2 cups chicken broth
- 1 cup uncooked rice
- 1 egg, beaten
- ¾ cup crumbled feta cheese
- Salt and pepper to taste

Heat the olive oil slightly over medium heat in heavy saucepan. Add the onion, parsley, and walnuts. Cook over medium heat for about 10 minutes or until onion wilts and loses its juice. Add the ground beef and cook for about 20 minutes. Stir in the cumin, cinnamon, mint, chicken broth, and rice. Cover and cook about 30 minutes or until rice is done. Remove from heat, stir in egg and feta cheese, and taste for seasoning. Add salt and pepper as needed. Place in pie shell, cap, and finish as described on pages 17-18. Bake as directed above or until golden.

PATCHWORK PIE

One of my first recipes for MOM and still a favorite. Serve with sour cream and guacamole salad. Eat hot or cold. Easy to make, full of nutrition, and perfect for parties or for a family dinner.

PREHEAT OVEN: 500°F.

PASTRY NEEDED: Unbaked 9-inch double-crust pie.

BAKING TIME: 15 minutes at 500°F, 35 to 40 minutes at 350°F.

SERVINGS: 4 to 6.
May be frozen unbaked.

- 1½ pounds ground beef
- ¼ cup shredded carrots
- ½ cup shredded onion
- 1 cup whole canned tomatoes, with juice
- 3 tablespoons chili powder
- ⅛ teaspoon oregano
- ½ teaspoon hot red pepper flakes
- 1 cup cooked rice (white or brown)
- 1 cup shredded zucchini
- 4 cloves garlic, minced
- 2 tablespoons tomato paste
- ½ teaspoon cumin
- 1 tablespoon Tabasco (less if desired)
- Salt and pepper to taste

Place all ingredients in a medium-size bowl and mix with hands or wooden spoon until well blended. Place in pie shell, cap and finish as described on pages 17-18. Bake as directed above or until golden.

BEEF BRASILIA PIE

An American version of the Brasilian national dish feijoada. *I serve it with a sliced orange and red onion salad on a bed of greens.*

PREHEAT OVEN: 500°F.

PASTRY NEEDED: Unbaked 9-inch double-crust pie.

BAKING TIME: 15 minutes at 500°F, 20 minutes at 375°F.

SERVINGS: 4 to 6.

May be frozen unbaked.

2 **cups dried black beans**
   Salted water
¼ **pound salt pork, diced**
2 **pounds lean beef, cubed (either brisket or stewing beef)**
¼ **pound smoked tongue, peeled and cubed**
½ **pound chorizos, sliced (or other Spanish sausage)**
1 **whole orange, quartered**
4 **cloves garlic, minced**
1 **medium-sized onion, diced**
2 **bay leaves**

Place the beans in a large Dutch oven and add enough salted water to cover. Soak for at least 6 hours. Drain, rinse, cover with fresh water, and bring to boil. Cook for about 1½ hours or until beans are beginning to get tender.

In a frying pan over medium heat, brown the salt pork until it has rendered most of its fat. Add the beef and cook until well browned. Stir in the smoked tongue and chorizos, then add to the black beans, along with the quartered orange, garlic, onion, and bay leaves. Stir and cook, covered, over medium heat for about 45 minutes.

Remove from heat and discard orange and bay leaves. Take out 1 cup of beans, mash them, and stir back into the mixture. Taste for seasoning and pour into pie shell. Cap and finish as described on pages 17-18. Bake as directed above or until golden.

BEEF AND BEER PIE

A Belgian stew called carbonnade *is the base for this pie. Beer gives body to the sauce that is different from the expected beef and red wine. A terrific crowd-pleaser, great for buffet parties. Just have plenty of ice-cold beer or cider on hand.*

PREHEAT OVEN: 500°F.

PASTRY NEEDED: Unbaked 9-inch double-crust pie.

BAKING TIME: 15 minutes at 500°F, 20 minutes at 375°F.

SERVINGS: 4 to 6.

May be frozen unbaked.

¼ **pound fatback, cubed**
2½ **pounds lean stewing beef, cubed**
1 **cup chopped onion**
   Salt and pepper to taste
4 **cloves garlic, mashed**
1 **tablespoon minced fresh parsley**
1 **cup beef stock**
3 **cups beer**
3 **tablespoons brown sugar**
½ **teaspoon thyme**
3 **tablespoons butter**
4 **tablespoons flour**

Place the fatback in a large, heavy saucepan or Dutch oven. Cook over medium heat until fatback is like cracklings and all fat has been rendered. Remove the fatback and all but about 3 tablespoons of fat in the saucepan. Add the beef, onion, and salt and pepper to taste. Cook over medium heat until beef begins to lose its pink color and onions begin to wilt. Add the garlic, parsley, and beef stock, stirring until well blended. Add the beer, brown sugar, and thyme. Cover and cook over medium heat for approximately 1 hour, or until stew is done. Make a roux with the butter and flour and whisk into the beef stew. Cook over medium heat until sauce thickens a bit. Pour into pie shell, cap, and finish as described on pages 17-18. Bake as directed above or until golden.

OTHER MEATS

VEAL MARENGO PIE

When I prepare this as the traditional stew, I always make sure to have enough to use for pies. A tossed green salad, refreshing beverage, and poached oranges in red wine for dessert complete this company-perfect meal.

PREHEAT OVEN: 500°F.

PASTRY NEEDED: Unbaked 9-inch double-crust pie.

BAKING TIME: 15 minutes at 500°F, 20 minutes at 375°F.

SERVINGS: 4 to 6.
May be frozen unbaked.

```
 2  pounds veal stew meat, cubed
 4  tablespoons flour
    Salt and pepper to taste
 5  tablespoons olive oil
 1  large onion, minced
 1  cup seeded, chopped tomatoes
 2  tablespoons tomato paste
 1  clove garlic, minced
 ½  teaspoon tarragon
 ¼  teaspoon thyme
 ½  small orange, quartered
 1  cup white wine
12  whole small mushrooms
```

Dredge the veal with flour and salt and pepper. Pour olive oil into a heavy saucepan or Dutch oven over medium heat and add the veal. Cook, stirring frequently, until veal is browned on all sides. Remove veal from pot, pour off all but 1 tablespoon fat, and add onions, tomatoes, tomato paste, garlic, and herbs. Cook over low heat, stirring frequently, until onion begins to wilt. Add the orange quarters and wine and scrape to remove the brown bits from the bottom of the pan. Return veal to pot and add salt and pepper to taste. Cover and cook over medium heat about 30 minutes or until veal stew is done. Remove orange, stir in mushrooms, and pour into pie shell. Cap and finish as described on pages 17-18. Bake as directed above or until golden.

TWELFTH NIGHT PIE

A centuries-old English tradition, which used up all the leftover meats of the Christmas holiday. I have left out the wild boar and grouse and tried to make do with the more available American ham and turkey. A great finish to the holiday season.

PREHEAT OVEN: 500°F.

PASTRY NEEDED: Unbaked 9-inch double-crust pie.

BAKING TIME: 15 minutes at 500°F, 20 minutes at 375°F.

SERVINGS: 4 to 6.
May be frozen unbaked.

2 cups ground cooked ham
2 medium onions, minced
2 tablespoons melted butter
¼ teaspoon cinnamon
2 cups ground cooked turkey
2 stalks celery, minced
1 cup applesauce
¼ teaspoon celery seed
6 cooked link sausages

Place all ingredients except sausage links in a medium-size mixing bowl and stir to blend. Spread a thin layer on the bottom of pie shell. Arrange the 6 sausage links on the bottom layer so that each slice of pie will contain a sausage. Cover with remaining ground meat mixture, cap, and finish as described on pages 17-18. Bake as directed above or until golden.

SAUSAGE AND PEPPERS PIE

Instead of making a hero, hoagie, or submarine, put your sausage and peppers into a pie. Easy to do, delicious to eat, makes a great meal!

PREHEAT OVEN: 500°F.

PASTRY NEEDED: Unbaked 9-inch double-crust pie.

BAKING TIME: 15 minutes at 500°F, 20 minutes at 375°F.

SERVINGS: 4 to 6.
May be frozen unbaked.

1 pound Italian sweet sausage
1 pound Italian hot sausage
1 large onion, cubed
2 cloves garlic, minced
2 green peppers, seeded and sliced
1 teaspoon basil
¼ teaspoon oregano
2 cups canned crushed tomatoes

Cook the sausages, onion, and garlic in a heavy frying pan over medium heat, stirring frequently, until sausage loses its pink color. Add the green peppers, basil, and oregano. Cook for about 10 minutes or until peppers begin to wilt. Add the tomatoes, cover, and cook over medium heat for about 30 minutes or until the sauce is well flavored. Remove from heat and cool slightly. Pour into pie shell, cap, and finish as described on pages 17-18. Bake as directed above or until golden.

ZUPPA DI PIE

The pastry absorbs the flavors to achieve a wonderful taste. Serve at a buffet, or with a green salad and chilled wine or beer for a complete meal.

PREHEAT OVEN: 500°F.

PASTRY NEEDED: Unbaked 9-inch double-crust pie.

BAKING TIME: 15 minutes at 500°F, 20 minutes at 375°F.

SERVINGS: 4 to 6.
May be frozen unbaked.

1½ pounds hot Italian sausage
1½ pounds sweet Italian sausage
2 medium-size onions, cubed
6 cloves garlic, minced
1 tablespoon basil
½ teaspoon oregano
2 drops Tabasco
2 cups whole canned Italian tomatoes
¼ cup tomato paste

Cook the sausage meats, onions, and garlic in a large, heavy frying pan over medium heat, stirring frequently, until meat loses its pink color. Add the basil, oregano, Tabasco, tomatoes, and tomato paste. Cover and cook over medium heat for about 45 minutes or until sausage is well cooked and sauce is well flavored. Remove from heat and cool slightly. Pour into pie shell, cap, and finish as described on pages 17-18. Bake as directed above or until golden.

PORKLE PIE

A traditional combination of succulent pork and tart apples baked in a pastry shell. A perfect winter meal to serve with homemade applesauce, green beans vinaigrette, and ice-cold cider.

PREHEAT OVEN: 500°F.

PASTRY NEEDED: Unbaked 9-inch double-crust pie.

BAKING TIME: 15 minutes at 500°F, 20 minutes at 375°F.

SERVINGS: 4 to 6.
May be frozen unbaked.

¼	**pound bacon**
1	**large onion, chopped**
2½	**pounds lean pork, cubed**
2	**tablespoons flour**
	Salt and pepper
1	**large carrot, shredded**
½	**teaspoon sage**
¼	**teaspoon nutmeg**
½	**cup beer**
½	**cup cider**
½	**cup cream**
1½	**cups peeled, cored, and cut up Granny Smith apples**

Fry the bacon over medium heat in a heavy frying pan. When done, remove bacon, drain on paper towel, and set aside. Leave 3 tablespoons fat in the frying pan, add the chopped onion, and cook, stirring frequently, until onion begins to wilt. Dredge the pork with flour and salt and pepper. Place in frying pan with the onion and cook, stirring frequently, until pork is browned on all sides. Add the carrot, sage, nutmeg, beer, and cider. Cover and cook over medium heat for about 30 minutes or until pork is done. Remove from heat. Stir in cream, add salt and pepper to taste, return to heat, and cook for about 10 minutes or until sauce begins to thicken. Remove from heat, stir in bacon and apples, and pour into pie shell. Cap and finish as described on pages 17-18. Bake as directed above or until golden.

CANADIAN PORK PIE

Based on the French-Canadian tourtière, *this pie is a year-round favorite. It can be eaten hot or cold and makes a great lunch for brown baggers. If you don't have any leftover poultry, increase the pork to 2½ pounds.*

PREHEAT OVEN: 500°F.

PASTRY NEEDED: Unbaked 9-inch double-crust pie.

BAKING TIME: 15 minutes at 500°F, 20 minutes at 375°F.

SERVINGS: 4 to 6.
May be frozen unbaked.

1½	**pounds lean ground pork**
2	**stalks celery, diced**
¼	**teaspoon ground cloves**
¼	**teaspoon marjoram**
1	**egg**
1	**medium-size onion, minced**
1	**tablespoon minced fresh parsley**
¼	**teaspoon ground cinnamon**
2	**cups chopped, cooked poultry**
½	**cup bread crumbs**

Place all ingredients in a medium-size bowl and stir to blend. Place in pie shell, cap, and finish with a lattice crust as described on pages 17-18. Bake as directed above or until golden.

VEAL AND PEPPERS PIE

*The delicate flavor of veal combined with
the bright colors of green and red
peppers make a terrific pie.*

PREHEAT OVEN: 500°F.

PASTRY NEEDED: Unbaked 9-inch
double-crust pie.

BAKING TIME: 15 minutes at 500°F,
20 minutes at 375°F.

SERVINGS: 4 to 6.
May be frozen unbaked.

2 **pounds veal stew meat, cubed**
4 **tablespoons flour**
  Salt and pepper to taste
4 **to 6 tablespoons olive oil**
3 **green peppers, seeded and
  sliced**
3 **sweet red peppers, seeded and
  sliced**
1 **whole onion, minced**
½ **teaspoon basil**
2 **cups chicken broth**

*Exotic Veal and Peppers Pie
prepared with Mom's Flaky Pastry
and a creative Easy Woven Lattice Top.*

Dredge the veal with flour and salt
and pepper. Heat olive oil in a heavy
saucepan over medium heat. Add veal
and cook, turning frequently to brown
on all sides. Remove veal and drain
off all but 2 tablespoons fat. Add the
green and red peppers, onion, and
basil and stir until vegetables begin to
wilt. Sprinkle with salt and pepper to
taste. Add chicken broth and cook,
covered, over medium heat for about
20 minutes or until veal begins to be
done. If sauce is not thick enough,
make a roux of 3 tablespoons flour
and 2 tablespoons butter and whisk
in, a bit at a time. When a medium
gravy has been achieved, pour into
pie shell, cap, and finish as described
on pages 17-18. Bake as directed above
or until golden.

ITALIAN PORK PIE

*Another pie that is tasty either hot or cold.
For a gourmet meal, accompany it
with braised kale or Swiss chard,
crispy bread sticks, and
fresh fruit for dessert.*

PREHEAT OVEN: 500°F.

PASTRY NEEDED: Unbaked 9-inch
double-crust pie.

BAKING TIME: 15 minutes at 500°F,
20 minutes at 375°F.

SERVINGS: 4 to 6.
May be frozen unbaked.

2 **pounds lean ground pork**
2 **tablespoons fresh rosemary,
  chopped**
1 **cup bread crumbs**
2 **Italian sweet sausages, casings
  removed**
1 **tablespoon chopped Italian
  parsley**
1 **large onion, grated**
  Salt and pepper to taste
½ **cup grated Parmesan cheese**

Place all ingredients except the
Parmesan cheese in a mixing bowl
and stir to blend. Sprinkle ¼ cup
grated Parmesan cheese in the bottom
of pie shell. Spread the pork mixture
on top of the cheese, sprinkle with remaining Parmesan, cap, and finish as
described on pages 17-18. Bake as
directed above or until golden.

SCOT'S LAMB PIE

*Made with leftover leg of lamb,
this pie is one of the tastiest leftovers I know.
You may also use stewing lamb if you
brown it and cook slightly before
you proceed with the general recipe.*

PREHEAT OVEN: 500°F.
PASTRY NEEDED: Unbaked 9-inch
double-crust pie.
BAKING TIME: 15 minutes at 500°F,
20 minutes at 375°F.
SERVINGS: 4 to 6.
May be frozen unbaked.

¼ pound butter
1 tablespoon vegetable oil
¾ pound chicken livers
4 tablespoons flour
1 large onion, chopped
¼ cup chicken broth
½ cup water
¼ cup sherry
Salt and pepper to taste
¼ teaspoon thyme
⅛ teaspoon rosemary
2 cups cubed cooked lamb
1½ cups frozen petit peas

Melt butter and vegetable oil in heavy frying pan over medium heat. Dredge the chicken livers in flour and brown in melted butter over medium heat. Add the onion and cook, stirring frequently, until onion wilts. Add the chicken broth, water, sherry, salt and pepper, and herbs to the frying pan, stirring frequently to mix. Remove from heat. Stir in the lamb and the peas. Mix to blend. Pour into pie shell, cap, and finish as described on pages 17-18. Bake as directed above or until golden.

CROSTADA

*The combination of Italian cheeses and
meats creates a zesty main-course pie.*

PREHEAT OVEN: 375°F.
PASTRY NEEDED: Unbaked 9-inch
pie shell.
BAKING TIME: 25 to 30 minutes.
SERVINGS: 6 to 8.

8 ounces salami or other Italian
sandwich meat, thinly sliced
and cut into strips
½ cup sliced black olives
¾ cup Italian plum tomatoes,
peeled, seeded, and chopped
1 tablespoon minced fresh parsley
1 teaspoon flour
Salt and pepper to taste
Pinch oregano
½ cup grated Romano or Parmesan
cheese
½ cup grated Italian Fontina
cheese
3 eggs
1½ cups cream

Combine all ingredients except the eggs and cream and stir to mix. Beat the eggs and cream together in a medium-size mixing bowl, add the salami mixture, and stir to mix. Pour into pie shell and bake as directed above.

RONNIE'S PAPA'S SAUSAGE PIE

An Italian friend's memories of his favorite childhood supper led to the creation of this pie. It is particularly suited to a late Sunday brunch with eggs, cheese, and meat as its main ingredients.

PREHEAT OVEN: 500°F.

PASTRY NEEDED: Unbaked 9-inch double-crust pie.

BAKING TIME: 15 minutes at 500°F, 20 minutes at 375°F.

SERVINGS: 4 to 6.
May be frozen unbaked.

6 **links Italian sausage**
4 **egg yolks**
1 **teaspoon pepper**
1 **pound ricotta cheese**
1 **cup Romano grated cheese**
½ **teaspoon salt**
4 **egg whites, whipped**
1 **teaspoon black pepper**
3 **teaspoons grated Parmesan cheese**

Remove the sausage meat from its casing and fry over medium heat in heavy frying pan until lightly browned, breaking it into pieces as it cooks. Remove from heat and drain. Mix together egg yolks, 1 teaspoon pepper, ricotta and Romano cheeses, and salt. Add the sausage and whipped egg whites, stir to blend, and pour into pie shell. Cap and finish as described on pages 17-18. Brush the top crust with milk, then sprinkle with coarsely ground black pepper and Parmesan cheese. Cut air vents and bake as directed above or until golden.

SEAFOOD

NEW ENGLAND CLAM PIE

This recipe came from a friend who summers on Nantucket and who relives his summer through typical New England recipes all winter long.

PREHEAT OVEN: 500°F.

PASTRY NEEDED: Unbaked 9-inch double-crust pie.

BAKING TIME: 15 minutes at 500°F, 20 minutes at 375°F.

SERVINGS: 4 to 6.
May be frozen unbaked.

3 **cups ground clams**
1 **cup oyster cracker crumbs**
1 **tablespoon minced parsley**
¼ **cup heavy cream**
   Dash of cayenne
⅓ **cup clam liquid**
2 **eggs, beaten**
2 **tablespoons melted butter**
½ **cup milk**

Mix all ingredients together in a medium-size mixing bowl. Place in pie shell, cap, and finish as described on pages 17-18. Bake as directed above or until golden.

PISSALADIÈRE

An open-faced tart that makes a perfect picnic pie. If you use Mediterranean black olives, watch out for the pits.

PREHEAT OVEN: 375°F.

PASTRY NEEDED: Baked 9-inch pie shell.

BAKING TIME: 10 minutes.

SERVINGS: 6.

6 tablespoons olive oil
6 cups chopped onion
2 cloves garlic, minced
1 large tomato, peeled, seeded, and chopped
1 tablespoon minced fresh parsley
⅛ teaspoon thyme
Salt and pepper to taste
10 anchovy filets
1 cup whole Mediterranean black olives or regular black olives, pitted and sliced

Pissaladière made with Mom's Flaky Pastry and trimmed with a cutout scalloped edge.

Bring the olive oil to near smoking in heavy frying pan. Lower heat and add the onions and garlic, stirring frequently. Cover and cook over low heat for about 15 minutes. Uncover and cook for about 45 minutes or until the onions are very tender but not brown. Toward the end of the cooking add the tomato, parsley, thyme, and salt and pepper. Stir to mix. Pour the onion mixture into the baked pastry shell. Arrange the anchovies and olives in a pattern on the top and bake as directed above. Let set about 10 minutes before cutting.

LOBSTER PIE

This pie is very rich so you might want to serve small portions.

PREHEAT OVEN: 500°F.

PASTRY NEEDED: Unbaked 9-inch double-crust pie.

BAKING TIME: 15 minutes at 500°F, 20 minutes at 375°F.

SERVINGS: 4 to 6.
May be frozen unbaked.

6 tablespoons butter
¼ cup minced shallots
1 tablespoon minced fresh parsley
¼ cup flour
3 cups milk (or 2 cups fish stock and 1 cup milk)
Salt and pepper to taste
1 egg yolk
3 cups cooked lobster meat
1½ cups chopped fresh mushrooms

In a heavy saucepan over medium heat, melt the butter. Add the shallots and parsley and cook until shallots begin to wilt. Stir in the flour, then add the 3 cups liquid, and salt and pepper to taste and cook, stirring, until a medium sauce has been formed. Put the egg yolk in a small bowl and whisk in a small amount of the sauce. Then combine with mixture in saucepan and whisk until blended. Stir in the lobster and mushrooms and pour into pie shell. Cap and finish as described on pages 17-18. Bake as directed above or until golden.

CHOWDER PIE

New England- or Manhattan-style, whole clams or chopped, everyone has his or her favorite recipe for clam chowder. For a change of pace try wrapping your chowder in pastry. Delicious! You can also substitute flaked fish for the clams.

PREHEAT OVEN: 500°F.

PASTRY NEEDED: Unbaked 9-inch double-crust pie.

BAKING TIME: 15 minutes at 500°F, 20 minutes at 375°F.

SERVINGS: 4 to 6.
May be frozen unbaked.

 2 **cups chopped clams with liquid**
 ½ **pound salt pork, diced**
 1 **large onion, diced**
 3 **tablespoons flour**
 2 **cups heavy cream or milk, approximately**
   Salt and pepper to taste
 ¼ **teaspoon dried thyme**
   Dash cayenne
 2 **cups diced cooked potatoes**

Drain the clams, reserving the liquid, and set aside. In a heavy frying pan over medium heat, cook the salt pork until well browned. Remove from pan with slotted spoon and discard. Cook the onion in the pork fat over medium heat until it begins to wilt. Stir in flour and mix until well blended. Combine reserved clam liquid with enough heavy cream to make 2½ cups liquid. Stir into flour mixture along with the salt and pepper and thyme and blend well. Add a dash of cayenne, stir, and remove from heat. Mix in clams and potatoes, pour into pie shell, cap, and finish as described on pages 17-18. Bake as directed above or until golden.

OYSTER PIE

A different yet delectable way to use oysters. When you serve it, keep the rest of the menu light.

PREHEAT OVEN: 500°F.

PASTRY NEEDED: Unbaked 9-inch double-crust pie.

BAKING TIME: 15 minutes at 500°F, 20 minutes at 375°F.

SERVINGS: 4 to 6.
May be frozen unbaked.

 3 **cups oysters with liquid**
 6 **tablespoons butter**
 3 **tablespoons flour**
 2 **cups heavy cream, approximately**
 2 **egg yolks**
 1 **tablespoon Madeira**
   Dash nutmeg
 1 **cup quartered artichoke hearts**

Drain the oysters, reserving the liquid, and set aside. In heavy saucepan melt the butter, stir in the flour, and mix. Combine the reserved oyster liquid and enough heavy cream to make 2½ cups. Add to saucepan and stir over medium heat until consistency of a light cream sauce. Put the 2 egg yolks in a small mixing bowl and quickly whisk in a bit of the cream sauce. Stir this back into the sauce, add the Madeira and nutmeg, and mix. Add the oysters and the artichoke hearts, pour into pie shell, cap, and finish as described on pages 17-18. Bake as directed above or until golden.

CIOPPINO

A fish stew, Italian in origin, that I adapted for a pie. You may use whatever fish and/or seafood you prefer.

PREHEAT OVEN: 500°F.

PASTRY NEEDED: Unbaked 9-inch double-crust pie.

BAKING TIME: 15 minutes at 500°F, 20 minutes at 375°F.

SERVINGS: 4 to 6.
May be frozen unbaked.

4 tablespoons olive oil
1 large onion, chopped
½ cup seeded and chopped green pepper
3 cloves garlic, minced
3 cups canned Italian tomatoes
½ cup tomato sauce
½ cup red wine
3 tablespoons chopped parsley
½ teaspoon basil
½ teaspoon oregano
Salt and pepper to taste
2 pounds of any mixture of the following: fish filets cut into chunks, scallops, lobster, clams, shrimp, squid

Place the olive oil in a heavy saucepan over medium heat. Add the onion, green pepper, and garlic. Stirring frequently, cook until vegetables are wilted. Add remaining ingredients, except seafood, and bring to a boil. Lower heat, cover, and cook for about 30 minutes. Remove from heat, add the seafood (any large pieces cut into chunks), and pour into pie shell. Cap and finish as described on pages 17-18. Bake as directed above or until golden.

VEGETARIAN AND QUICHE

KAZOOTIE PIE

Why the name? I don't know. We made it up on a day when we were having fun in the kitchen. This is simple to make, absolutely delicious, and a great lunch, brunch, or appetizer as well as a main-course pie.

PREHEAT OVEN: 500°F.

PASTRY NEEDED: Unbaked 9-inch double-crust pie.

BAKING TIME: 15 minutes at 500°F, 20 minutes at 375°F.

SERVINGS: 8 to 10 as an appetizer; 4 to 6 as a main course.
May be frozen unbaked.

2¼ cups grated Fontina cheese
2 cups grated raw zucchini

In a pie shell place a layer of cheese, a layer of zucchini, a second layer of cheese, a second layer of zucchini, and top with a light layer of cheese. Finish with a lattice top, page 17. Bake as directed above or until golden, and serve warm, not hot.

GERMAN ONION PIE

Serve this for brunch, lunch, or as a side dish. For a heartier dish add about ½ pound bacon or sausage, cooked and crumbled, and present as a main course.

PREHEAT OVEN: 500°F.

PASTRY NEEDED: Unbaked 9-inch double-crust pie.

BAKING TIME: 10 minutes at 500°F, 35 to 45 minutes at 350°F.

SERVINGS: 4 to 6.
May be frozen uncooked.

4 tablespoons unsalted (sweet) butter
3 cups chopped onion
4 eggs, beaten
1 cup sour cream
2 tablespoons chopped scallion greens
¼ teaspoon caraway seed
   Pinch of nutmeg

Melt the butter in a heavy frying pan over medium heat. Add the onion and cook for about 10 minutes or until wilted. Remove from heat and cool slightly. In a medium-size mixing bowl blend the eggs, sour cream, scallion greens, caraway, and nutmeg. Stir in the onion and pour into pie shell. Finish with lattice top as described on pages 17-18. Bake as directed above or until golden.

ZUCCHINI PIE

A perfect side dish, or add ham, cooked bacon, or sausage and you have dinner.

PREHEAT OVEN: 500°F.

PASTRY NEEDED: Unbaked 9-inch double-crust pie.

BAKING TIME: 10 minutes at 500°F, 35 to 45 minutes at 350°F.

SERVINGS: 4 to 6.
May be frozen unbaked.

4 tablespoons unsalted (sweet) butter
1 tablespoon olive oil
¼ cup chopped onion
¼ cup seeded and chopped green pepper
3 cups cooked, sliced zucchini, well drained
3 eggs, beaten
¼ cup heavy cream
⅛ cup grated Parmesan cheese
½ tablespoon basil
   Dash of oregano
   Salt and pepper to taste

Melt the butter in a heavy saucepan over medium heat. Add the olive oil, onion, and green pepper and cook for about 15 minutes over low heat. Remove from heat and stir in remaining ingredients. Pour into pie shell, cap, and finish as described on pages 17-18. Bake as directed above or until golden.
Note: You may wish to reserve the cheese and basil and sprinkle on the top crust before baking.

NIRVANA PIE

Vegetables and brown rice combine to make a nutritious vegetarian meal in a pastry shell. If you don't like coriander, substitute any herb or spice that you prefer.

PREHEAT OVEN: 500°F.

PASTRY NEEDED: Unbaked 9-inch Whole Wheat Pastry pie shell (page 24) or any 9-inch pastry shell.

BAKING TIME: 15 minutes at 500°F, 20 minutes at 375°F.

SERVINGS: 4 to 6.
May be frozen unbaked.

2 cups assorted raw sliced vegetables (carrot, eggplant, sweet potato, cabbage, peppers, squash, turnip)
1 medium-size onion, diced
½ cup chopped greens (spinach, kale, mustard, etc.)
2 cups cooked brown rice
½ cup orange juice
½ cup canned Italian tomatoes
1 teaspoon ground coriander
¼ teaspoon ground orange peel
¼ teaspoon ground cumin
   Salt and pepper to taste

In a medium-size mixing bowl combine all ingredients and stir until well blended. Mound in pie shell, cap, and finish as described on pages 17-18. Bake as directed above or until golden.

Nirvana Pie baked in Whole Wheat Pastry. The moons and stars were cut out from the pastry and then positioned on the top and edge.

RATATOUILLE PIE

*One of my favorite midsummer lunches
when the vegetables are at their peak.
Serve with a garnish made from
chopped parsley, capers, and anchovies;
a tossed green salad; and iced tea,
iced coffee, or wine.*

PREHEAT OVEN: 500°F.

PASTRY NEEDED: Unbaked 9-inch
double-crust pie.

BAKING TIME: 10 minutes at 500°F,
15 minutes at 350°F.

SERVINGS: 4 to 6.
May be frozen unbaked.

¾ cup olive oil
1 large onion, chopped
1 clove garlic, minced
1 large eggplant, peeled and
   cubed
2 cups cubed zucchini
1 sweet pepper, seeded and
   cubed
2 cups peeled, seeded, and cubed
   tomatoes
1 tablespoon fresh basil, chopped
   Salt and pepper to taste
1 teaspoon red wine vinegar

Place the olive oil in a heavy frying
pan over medium heat. Add the
onion and garlic and cook for about
10 minutes over low heat until onion
begins to wilt. Stir in the eggplant and
cook for about 5 minutes. Add the
zucchini, sweet pepper, and tomatoes
and cook for about 5 minutes. Add
the basil, salt and pepper, and vinegar
and stir to blend. Cover and cook
over medium heat for about 30
minutes or until vegetables have
cooked down a bit. If the ratatouille
has too much liquid, remove cover
and cook until juice has been
reduced. Pour into pie shell and
finish with a lattice top as described
on pages 17-18. Then bake as directed
above or until golden.

GREEK SPINACH
PIE

*Like most Greek pastries, spinach pie
is usually made with filo dough, but this has
been adapted to our traditional pastry.
It makes an excellent main course.*

PREHEAT OVEN: 500°F.

PASTRY NEEDED: Unbaked 9-inch
double-crust pie.

BAKING TIME: 10 minutes at 500°F,
20 minutes at 350°F.

SERVINGS: 4 to 6.
May be frozen unbaked.

4 cups cooked chopped spinach
3 tablespoons butter
½ cup grated onion
2 cloves garlic, minced
4 eggs
   Salt and pepper to taste
¼ teaspoon nutmeg
1½ cups crumbled feta cheese

Place spinach in strainer and press
out excess liquid. Combine spinach
with remaining ingredients, except
feta cheese, and blend well. Gently stir
in the feta cheese and taste for seasoning. Pour into pie shell, cap, and
finish as described on pages 17-18.
Bake as directed above or until golden.

WIZARD PIE

I use as many different vegetables as I can in this, but if you're limited to only two or three, make sure that you include eggplant and carrots, sweet potato, or winter squash. This will balance the texture, moisture, and taste of the pie, which is also a terrific dish for those on salt-free diets. I like it highly seasoned, but you can reduce the spiciness by eliminating the hot pepper flakes and adding just a drop of Tabasco sauce.

PREHEAT OVEN: 500°F.

PASTRY NEEDED: Unbaked 9-inch double-crust pie.

BAKING TIME: 15 minutes at 500°F, 35 to 45 minutes at 350°F.

SERVINGS: 8 to 10 as an appetizer; 4 to 6 as a main course. May be frozen uncooked.

1 medium-size onion, chopped
2 cloves garlic, crushed
½ cup unsweetened wheat germ
1 cup crushed tomatoes with juice
1 teaspoon dried basil or 1 tablespoon fresh
⅛ teaspoon hot pepper flakes Tabasco sauce to taste
4 cups raw shredded vegetables, which may include any mixture of the following: carrots, squash (winter or summer), sweet potato, celery, green and red peppers, spinach, kale, Swiss chard, turnips, parsnips, rutabaga, broccoli, eggplant, and cabbage

Mix all ingredients in a bowl and stir to blend. Taste for seasoning. Mound mixture in a pie shell, cap, and finish as described on pages 17-18. Bake as directed above or until golden. (Any leftover filling can be used for empanadas or turnovers. See pages 67 and 120, 121.)

CORN PIE

Best in August when the corn is sweet and tender, yet it's still good throughout the year using canned corn.

PREHEAT OVEN: 475°F.

PASTRY NEEDED: Unbaked 9-inch double-crust pie.

BAKING TIME: 15 minutes at 475°F, 30 minutes at 325°F.

SERVINGS: 4 to 6. May be frozen unbaked.

2 cups whole-kernel corn (drained if canned)
4 tablespoons unsalted (sweet) butter, melted
4 eggs, beaten
1 cup grated cheddar cheese
½ cup heavy cream
1 tablespoon green pepper, minced
Salt and pepper to taste

Mix all ingredients together in medium-size mixing bowl. Pour into pie shell, cap, and finish as described on pages 17-18. Or bake as an open-faced pie. Bake as directed above or until golden.

BASIC QUICHE

Before Julia Child, quiches were almost unknown in America. Now this open-faced custard pie is routinely served and can even be found in the freezer section of the neighborhood grocery store. One of the easiest pies to make and certainly one of the most versatile. Serve at breakfast, lunch, dinner, or for snacks with any filling you choose.

PREHEAT OVEN: 375°F

PASTRY NEEDED: Unbaked 9-inch pie shell.

BAKING TIME: 25 to 30 minutes.

SERVINGS: 6 to 8.

 3 **eggs**
1½ **cups cream**
 ½ **cup Gruyère cheese, grated**
 1 **tablespoon unsalted (sweet) butter, cut into bits**
    Pinch each of white pepper and nutmeg
    Salt to taste

Beat the eggs and cream together. Add the remaining ingredients and stir to blend. Pour into pie shell and bake as directed above or until set.

VARIATIONS

You may add any of the following to the above ingredients:

 ½ **pound cooked bacon, crumbled (Quiche Lorraine)**
 ½ **pound cooked sausage, crumbled**
 ⅓ **to ½ pound cooked ham, diced**
 1 **cup minced, drained clams**
 1 **to 1½ cups cooked spinach, chopped, plus ⅛ teaspoon dill**
 ½ **cup cooked asparagus, chopped (or place 6 or 8 whole asparagus stalks in a pie-serving pattern so each portion has one whole stalk)**

OTHER VARIATIONS

TOMATO QUICHE

 2 **tablespoons butter**
 2 **tablespoons olive oil**
 2 **tablespoons grated onion**
 2 **cups peeled, seeded, and chopped tomato**
 ½ **teaspoon basil**
    Dash of Tabasco
 1 **Basic Quiche recipe**

Melt butter in heavy saucepan, add oil and grated onion, and stir to mix. Cook 5 minutes over medium heat, stirring frequently. Add tomato, basil, and Tabasco and cook for 10 to 15 minutes, or until some of the liquid has evaporated. Combine with Basic Quiche mixture, pour into unbaked pie shell, and bake as directed.

Tomato Quiche baked in Mom's Flaky Pastry.

ONION QUICHE

3 tablespoons butter
1 tablespoon olive oil
3 cups diced onion
1 Basic Quiche recipe

Melt butter in heavy saucepan. Add the olive oil and onion and cook, covered, over very low heat for 30 to 45 minutes, or until onion is well cooked but not brown. Combine with Basic Quiche mixture, pour into unbaked pie shell, and bake as directed.

BROCCOLI QUICHE

3 tablespoons butter
2 tablespoons grated onion
1 to 1½ cups chopped, cooked
  broccoli, well drained
1 Basic Quiche recipe

Melt butter in a small, heavy frying pan, add the onion, and cook over low heat for about 15 minutes. Stir in broccoli. Combine with Basic Quiche mixture, pour into unbaked pie shell, and bake as directed.

MUSHROOM QUICHE

3 tablespoons butter
1 tablespoon olive oil
2 cups sliced raw mushrooms
⅛ teaspoon thyme
1 Basic Quiche recipe

Melt butter in heavy saucepan. Add the olive oil, mushrooms, and thyme. Cook over low heat for about 15 minutes, or until mushrooms begin to lose much of their moisture. Raise heat and cook for 5 minutes more, until some of the moisture has begun to evaporate. Combine with Basic Quiche mixture, pour into unbaked pie shell, and bake as directed.

NIÇOISE QUICHE

Add 1 minced garlic clove, 8 to 10 chopped anchovy filets, and ½ cup pitted Mediterranean black olives to the Tomato Quiche recipe and proceed as described above.

ZUCCHINI QUICHE

3 tablespoons butter
2 tablespoons grated onion
2 cups grated zucchini
1 Basic Quiche recipe

Melt butter in heavy saucepan, add onion, and cook over medium heat for about 10 minutes, or until onion has begun to lose its moisture. Stir in zucchini and cook for 5 minutes. Combine with Basic Quiche mixture, pour into unbaked pie shell, and bake as directed.

SHRIMP, CRAB, OR LOBSTER QUICHE

3 tablespoons butter
3 tablespoons minced shallots
1 to 1½ cups shellfish
1 Basic Quiche recipe

Melt butter in heavy saucepan. Add shallots and cook over medium heat for about 10 minutes. Stir in shellfish and mix well. Combine with Basic Quiche mixture, pour into unbaked pie shell, and bake as directed.

TORTA RUSTICA

*Usually made with yeast dough,
this hearty Italian filling may be baked
as a double-crust pie or in a
pastry-lined lasagne pan.
It can also be made into individual
turnovers for lunches or picnics.*

PREHEAT OVEN: 500°F.

PASTRY NEEDED: Unbaked 9-inch
double-crust pie.

BAKING TIME: 15 minutes at 500°F,
20 to 30 minutes at 375°F.

SERVINGS: 6 to 8.

  3 **tablespoons olive oil**
  ½ **cup grated onion**
  1 **clove garlic, minced**
  2 **cups cooked chopped spinach**
  1 **cup ricotta cheese**
  ½ **cup grated Romano cheese**
    Salt and pepper to taste

Heat olive oil in a small frying pan
and add the onion and garlic. Cook for
about 15 minutes over medium heat
or until onion has wilted and absorbed
some of the oil. Place spinach in
strainer and press out excess liquid.
Combine spinach and cheeses in a
mixing bowl, add the onion and salt
and pepper, and stir to mix. Pour into
pie shell, cap, and finish as described
on pages 17-18. Bake as directed above
or until golden.

APPETIZERS

EMPANADAS

*Latin American "sandwiches"—great
cocktail party treats, terrific first
course, or easy lunch or picnic food.
The filling for Cubaña Pie
(page 43) can also be used in these.*

PREHEAT OVEN: 450°F.

PASTRY NEEDED: 12 unbaked 5-inch
pastry rounds (made from a 2-crust
pie recipe).

BAKING TIME: 10 minutes at 450°F,
20 minutes at 325°F.

SERVINGS: Makes 12 empanadas.
May be frozen unbaked.

  3 **tablespoons olive oil**
  ½ **cup grated onion**
  1 **clove garlic, minced**
  ¼ **cup pine nuts**
  ¼ **cup chopped pimiento-stuffed**
    green olives
  ½ **pound lean ground beef**
  ½ **teaspoon red pepper flakes**
  ½ **teaspoon cumin**
    Dash cinnamon
  ½ **cup raisins, soaked for 10**
    minutes in 1 cup boiling
    water (optional)
    Egg wash (page 18)

Place the olive oil in heavy frying pan
over medium heat. Add the onion
and garlic and cook for about 15
minutes or until moisture has begun
to evaporate. Add the pine nuts and
olives and cook, stirring frequently,
for about 5 minutes. Add the ground
beef and the seasonings and cook,
still stirring frequently, until beef
loses its pink color. If using raisins,
drain them and add to mixture now.
Put equal amounts of filling on each
of the 12 pastry rounds. Brush cold
water halfway around edge and fold
the pastry round in half to make a
crescent-shaped packet, crimping the
edges with your fingers or a fork.
Place on baking sheet, brush with egg
wash, and prick air vents in tops. Bake
as directed above or until golden.

PASTIES

The "sandwiches" of the British Isles.

PREHEAT OVEN: 450°F.

PASTRY NEEDED: 12 unbaked 5-inch pastry rounds (made from a 2-crust pie recipe).

BAKING TIME: 10 minutes at 450°F, 20 minutes at 350°F.

SERVINGS: 12 as an appetizer; 6 as a luncheon dish.
May be frozen unbaked.

- 5 **tablespoons butter**
- ½ **pound lean beef, diced**
- ¼ **cup diced raw potato**
- ¼ **cup diced carrot**
- 3 **tablespoons grated onion**
- 1 **tablespoon minced parsley**
  Salt and pepper to taste
- 1 **tablespoon flour**
- ½ **to ¾ cup beef broth**

Melt 3 tablespoons butter in a small saucepan over medium heat. Add the beef, cover, and cook for about 15 to 20 minutes or until beef has lost all its pink color. Add the potato, carrot, onion, parsley, and salt and pepper to taste. Cover and cook until meat mixture is well done. In a small frying pan melt remaining 2 tablespoons butter, stir in the flour, and add enough beef broth to make a sauce thick enough to bind meat mixture. Remove both sauce and meat from heat. Place meat mixture in a small bowl and mix in half the sauce. Divide meat mixture among the twelve pastry rounds and if necessary add a bit more sauce to each. Brush the edges with water and fold rounds in half to make a crescent shape. Crimp the edges with your finger or a fork. Brush the pasties with egg wash, if you wish, and prick air holes. Place on baking sheet and bake as directed above or until golden.

PIROZHKI

Russian in origin, these filled buns are traditionally made with yeast dough but they adapt well to our pastry. You will want to make the pastry rounds a bit thicker than usual so that they will hold a bun shape.

PREHEAT OVEN: 450°F.

PASTRY NEEDED: 12 unbaked 5-inch pastry rounds (made from a 2-crust pie recipe).

BAKING TIME: 10 minutes at 450°F, 15 minutes at 325°F.

SERVINGS: 12 as an appetizer; 6 as a main course.
May be frozen unbaked.

MEAT FILLING

- 2 **tablespoons butter**
- ¼ **cup minced onion**
- ¾ **pound lean ground beef or veal**
  Salt and pepper to taste
- 2 **tablespoons beef broth**
- 2 **hard-cooked eggs, chopped**
- 2 **tablespoons sour cream**
- 1 **tablespoon chopped dill**

Melt butter in small frying pan over medium heat. Add onion and the ground beef. Cook, stirring frequently, until meat has lost its pink color. Remove from heat. Add remaining ingredients and stir to mix.

Pasties baked in Mom's Flaky Pastry. For an interesting effect, vary the decorative trim.

CABBAGE FILLING

- 2 **tablespoons butter**
- ¼ **cup grated onion**
- 2 **cups finely shredded cabbbage**
- 2 **tablespoons chopped dill**
  Salt and pepper to taste
- ¼ **cup sour cream**
- 2 **hard-cooked eggs, chopped**

Melt butter in small frying pan over medium heat. Add the onion and cabbage, cover, lower heat, and cook until cabbage is well done. Remove from heat, add the remaining ingredients, and mix to blend.

For both recipes

Place an equal amount of filling in the center of each 5-inch pastry round. Brush the edges of the rounds with water and bring edges up to form bundle shape. Press edges together to make a secure packet, making certain that it is well sealed, and turn over so that the smooth side is on top. (They will look like little bundles.) Place on baking sheet, brush with egg wash, if you wish, and prick air holes. Bake as directed above or until golden.

HOBOS

Hobos are so named because they look like a hobo's sack.

PREHEAT OVEN: 450°F.

PASTRY NEEDED: 12 unbaked 5-inch pastry squares (made from a 2-crust pie recipe).

BAKING TIME: 10 minutes at 450°F, 10 minutes at 350°F.

SERVINGS: 12.
May be frozen unbaked.

- 4 **tablespoons butter**
- 1 **medium-size onion, grated**
- 1 **large potato, grated**
- 1 **large carrot, grated**
- 1 **tablespoon parsley, minced**
- ¾ **cup beef or chicken broth**
- 1 to 1½ **cups finely chopped cooked meat or poultry**
  Salt and pepper to taste
- 1 **egg, beaten (if needed)**

Melt the butter in a heavy saucepan over medium heat. Add the onion and cook for about 10 minutes. Add the potato, carrot, and parsley and cook, covered, over low heat for about 15 minutes or until vegetables have begun to lose their crispness. Add the stock and meat and stir to mix. Cook for about 5 more minutes until you have a well-blended, hashlike filling. Add salt and pepper to taste. If your mixture is too dry you may want to add part of a beaten egg to give it moisture. Put equal amounts of the filling in the center of each of the pastry squares. Moisten the edges of the squares with water. Bring the four corners up to meet at the center over the filling. Press together, crimp the new edges of the square, and if you have enough pastry, make little tie-like folds at the top of the hobo. Brush, if you wish, with egg wash or melted butter. Bake as directed above or until golden.

Chapter

DESSERT PIES

Four

FRUIT

MOM'S APPLE PIE

The all-American favorite. My only deviation from the norm is to lessen the sugar content. If the apples are particularly tart you may want to add a bit more sugar than I do.

PREHEAT OVEN: 450°F.

PASTRY NEEDED: Unbaked 9-inch double-crust pie.

BAKING TIME: 15 minutes at 450°F, 30 minutes at 350°F.

SERVINGS: 6 to 8.

2½ pounds Granny Smith or other tart green apples, peeled, cored, and thickly sliced
¼ to ½ cup sugar (to taste)
2 tablespoons flour
1 teaspoon cinnamon
¼ teaspoon grated lemon rind
½ teaspoon lemon juice
2 tablespoons unsalted (sweet) butter, cut into bits

Mix all ingredients with the apples. Place in pie shell. Cap and finish as described on pages 17-18. Bake as directed above or until golden.

Mom's Apple Crumb Pie made with Mom's Flaky Pastry and trimmed with a braided edge. Simple to make, but uncommonly delicious.

VARIATIONS

DUTCH APPLE PIE

Prepare the same recipe as above, but cut large vents in top crust. Seven minutes before pie is done remove from oven and pour ½ cup heavy cream into the pie through the vents. Return to oven and complete baking. Let pie set about 10 minutes before cutting.

APPLE CRUMB PIE

Prepare the same basic recipe, but instead of a pastry crust on top, cover with crumb topping. In a small mixing bowl combine ¾ cup flour, ½ cup brown sugar, ½ cup butter, and 1 teaspoon cinnamon, blending with your fingers until mixture is crumbly. Sprinkle over top of pie and bake 10 minutes at 450°F, 30 minutes at 375°F.

HARVEST APPLE PIE

Dried fruits, tart apples, and chopped nuts baked between two crusts for a scrumptious winter holiday pie.

PREHEAT OVEN: 450°F.

PASTRY NEEDED: Unbaked 9-inch double-crust pie.

BAKING TIME: 15 minutes at 450°F, 30 minutes at 350°F.

SERVINGS: 4 to 6.

2 pounds tart green cooking apples, peeled, cored, and thickly sliced
1 cup dark raisins
½ cup chopped dates
½ cup chopped nuts
½ cup brown sugar
2 tablespoons flour
2 tablespoons unsalted (sweet) butter, cut into bits
1 teaspoon cinnamon
½ teaspoon grated orange rind
¼ cup apple cider

Mix all ingredients together in a medium-size mixing bowl. Mound in the pie shell. Cap and finish as described on pages 17-18. Bake as directed above or until golden.

APPLE PECAN PIE

This open-faced nutty pie makes a very rich dessert, so you may wish to serve smaller pieces than usual. Top with whipped cream for a special treat.

PREHEAT OVEN: 450°F.

PASTRY NEEDED: Unbaked 9-inch pie shell.

BAKING TIME: 10 minutes at 450°F, 30 minutes at 350°F.

SERVINGS: 8 to 10.

¾ cup light brown sugar
½ cup unsalted (sweet) butter, cut into bits
½ cup dark corn syrup
4 eggs
1 teaspoon grated lemon peel
1½ cups peeled, cored, and coarsely chopped tart cooking apples
1½ cups chopped pecans

Beat the brown sugar, butter, and corn syrup together with an electric mixer. Add eggs and lemon peel and beat until well mixed. Stir in the apples and pecans, pour into pie shell, and bake as directed above or until golden. Let cool before serving.

APPLE SQUASH PIE

A terrific way to stretch a few apples and have a great dessert. Sweet potatoes make a good substitute for squash. Decrease the sweeteners and you have an unusual main-course side dish.

PREHEAT OVEN: 450°F.

PASTRY NEEDED: Unbaked 9-inch double-crust pie.

BAKING TIME: 15 minutes at 450°F, 40 minutes at 350°F.

SERVINGS: 6 to 8.

2 cups peeled, cored, and sliced tart cooking apples
2 cups peeled and sliced winter squash (or sweet potato)
½ cup honey
¼ cup brown sugar
3 tablespoons unsalted (sweet) butter, melted
¼ cup flour
1 teaspoon cinnamon
1 teaspoon nutmeg

Mix all ingredients together in a mixing bowl. Mound in a pie shell, cap, and finish as described on pages 17-18. Bake as directed above or until golden.

APPLE AND SOUR CREAM PIE

A rich and creamy apple pie.

PREHEAT OVEN: 400°F.

PASTRY NEEDED: Unbaked 9-inch double-crust pie.

BAKING TIME: 15 minutes at 400°F, 30 minutes at 350°F.

SERVINGS: 6 to 8.

2½ pounds tart green cooking apples, peeled, cored, and sliced
½ cup flour
½ cup sugar
1 teaspoon cinnamon
1 egg, beaten
1 cup sour cream
½ cup unsalted (sweet) butter, cut into chunks

Mix together all ingredients except butter, and pour into prepared pie shell. Scatter butter over top and finish with lattice top as described on page 17. Bake as directed above or until golden.

APPLE CHEESE PIE

The traditional slice of cheese with your apple has gone into the pie itself. The crust is cheesy and the filling is, too.

PREHEAT OVEN: 450°F.

PASTRY NEEDED: Cheddar cheese pastry for unbaked 9-inch double-crust pie (page 22).

BAKING TIME: 10 minutes at 450°F, 30 minutes at 350°F.

SERVINGS: 6 to 8.

2½ pounds tart green cooking apples, peeled, cored, and sliced
2 teaspoons lemon juice
¾ cup light brown sugar
2 tablespoons flour
1 teaspoon cinnamon
¼ teaspoon nutmeg
2 tablespoons unsalted (sweet) butter, cut into bits
¼ cup grated cheddar cheese

Mix the apples with all ingredients except cheddar cheese in medium-size bowl. Mound into pie shell, sprinkle with cheese, cap, and finish as described on pages 17-18. Bake as directed above or until golden.

APPLE CRANBERRY PIE

A favorite Thanksgiving pie with a beautiful color and taste combination.

PREHEAT OVEN: 450°F.

PASTRY NEEDED: Unbaked 9-inch double-crust pie.

BAKING TIME: 15 minutes at 450°F, 30 minutes at 350°F.

SERVINGS: 6 to 8.

3 cups peeled, cored, and sliced tart cooking apples
2 cups fresh whole cranberries
1 teaspoon grated lemon rind
2 tablespoons orange juice
⅔ cup sugar (or to taste)
3 tablespoons flour
¼ teaspoon cinnamon
¼ teaspoon nutmeg
2 tablespoons unsalted (sweet) butter

Mix all ingredients together in a medium-size mixing bowl. Pour into pie shell. Finish with a lattice top as described on page 17. Bake as directed above or until golden.

MARLBOROUGH PIE

This pie will keep you guessing, for it is almost impossible to identify as apple.

PREHEAT OVEN: 450°F.

PASTRY NEEDED: Unbaked 9-inch double-crust pie.

BAKING TIME: 15 minutes at 450°F, 15 to 20 minutes at 350°F.

SERVINGS: 6 to 8.

1 cup unsweetened homemade applesauce
1 cup sugar
4 eggs
¼ cup lemon juice
1 teaspoon grated lemon peel
   Dash of lemon juice
3 tablespoons unsalted (sweet) butter, melted

Beat all ingredients together in a medium-size mixing bowl. Pour into pie shell. Bake as directed above or until golden. Let cool before serving.

SWEET CHERRY PIE

Made with fresh Bing cherries, this pie is sensational. Test for sweetness before adding sugar so you don't add too much and thus lose the taste of the cherries.

PREHEAT OVEN: 425°F.

PASTRY NEEDED: Unbaked 9-inch double-crust pie.

BAKING TIME: 10 minutes at 425°F, 30 minutes at 375°F.

SERVINGS: 6 to 8.

4   cups pitted Bing cherries
2   tablespoons unsalted (sweet) butter, cut into bits
2   tablespoons flour
1   tablespoon lemon juice
1   teaspoon grated lemon rind
½   cup sugar, approximately

Mix all ingredients together in a medium-size mixing bowl. Pour into pie shell and finish with either closed top or lattice top, as described on page 15. Bake as directed above or until golden.

FRESH APRICOT PIE

A rare treat made only during those few short weeks of summer when apricots are ripe and juicy.

PREHEAT OVEN: 450°F.

PASTRY NEEDED: Unbaked 9-inch double-crust pie.

BAKING TIME: 10 minutes at 450°F, 30 minutes at 350°F.

SERVINGS: 6 to 8.

3   pounds ripe apricots, halved and pitted
2   drops almond extract (optional)
1   teaspoon lemon juice
1   tablespoon pineapple juice
½   cup sugar
2   tablespoons cornstarch
3   tablespoons unsalted (sweet) butter, melted
1   tablespoon sugar

Lay apricots in pie shell, cut side down. Beat together remaining ingredients, except for 1 tablespoon sugar, and pour mixture over apricots. Sprinkle with 1 tablespoon sugar, and finish with lattice top as described on page 17. Bake as directed above or until golden.

DRIED APRICOT AND PRUNE PIE

If you keep dried fruit on hand this is an easy pie to make on a moment's notice. Serve with a dollop of coffee ice cream on each slice.

PREHEAT OVEN: 450°F.

PASTRY NEEDED: Unbaked 9-inch double-crust pie.

BAKING TIME: 10 minutes at 450°F, 25 minutes at 350°F.

SERVINGS: 6 to 8.

2   cups whole pitted cooked prunes
1½ cups chopped dried apricots
½   cup chopped walnuts
⅓   cup sugar
1   teaspoon instant coffee powder
½   teaspoon cinnamon
¼   cup flour
¾   cup prune juice or apricot nectar
¼   cup unsalted (sweet) butter, melted

Mix all ingredients together in a medium-size mixing bowl. Pour into pie shell, cap, and finish as described on pages 17-18. Bake as directed above or until golden.

TWO-CRUST BERRY PIE

*Use just about any berry for this—
blueberries, blackberries, boysenberries,
dewberries, elderberries, gooseberries,
raspberries, or strawberries.*

PREHEAT OVEN: 450°F.

PASTRY NEEDED: Unbaked 9-inch
double-crust pie.

BAKING TIME: 10 minutes at 450°F,
30 minutes at 350°F.

SERVINGS: 6 to 8.

4 **cups fresh berries**
1 **cup sugar (more or less,**
    depending on berry used)
⅓ **cup flour**
1 **tablespoon lemon juice**
    Dash nutmeg
1 **teaspoon grated lemon rind**
2 **tablespoons unsalted (sweet)**
    butter, cut into bits

Mix all ingredients together and
pour into pie shell. Finish with either
closed top or lattice top, as described
on page 17. Bake as directed above or
until golden.

MINCEMEAT PIE

*This recipe will make enough filling for 12
to 15 pies. The extras can be taken
to a bake sale, or frozen for future use.
Or the mincemeat filling can be canned,
frozen, or refrigerated for up to six weeks.
If you are going to bake just one pie,
the following directions will hold.*

PREHEAT OVEN: 450°F.

PASTRY NEEDED: Unbaked 9-inch
double-crust pie.

BAKING TIME: 10 minutes at 450°F,
20 to 25 minutes at 350°F.

SERVINGS: 8 to 10.

1 **calf's tongue, skinned and**
    chopped fine
3 **pounds choice grade beef,**
    chopped fine
1 **pound suet, chopped fine**
3 **pounds black raisins**
3 **pounds currants**
3 **pounds mixed chopped glazed**
    fruit
8 **pounds apples, peeled, cored,**
    and chopped
    Grated rind of 2 lemons
    Grated rind of 2 oranges
4 **tablespoons ground cinnamon**
2 **tablespoons ground nutmeg**
1 **tablespoon ground cloves**
3 **pounds brown sugar**
4 **cups dry white wine**
6 to 8 **cups apple cider**
2 **cups apple brandy**

Mix all ingredients except the brandy
in a large, heavy Dutch oven. Cook
over very low heat for about 3 hours.
If additional liquid is required add
apple cider as needed. When mincemeat is a well-cooked, well-blended
mixture, stir in brandy and remove
from heat. Spoon 4 cups mincemeat
into pie shell, cap, and finish as
described on pages 17-18. Bake as
directed above or until golden.

PEACH BLUEBERRY PIE

One of my favorite summer combinations.
I always make a lattice top
so the beautiful color can show.

PREHEAT OVEN: 450°F.

PASTRY NEEDED: Unbaked 9-inch double-crust pie.

BAKING TIME: 10 minutes at 450°F, 30 minutes at 350°F.

SERVINGS: 6 to 8.

3 cups peeled, sliced fresh
   peaches (or nectarines)
2 cups blueberries
½ cup sugar
½ teaspoon nutmeg
3 tablespoons unsalted (sweet)
   butter, cut into bits
2 tablespoons flour
1 teaspoon grated lemon rind

Mix all ingredients together until well blended. Pour into pie shell and finish with lattice top as described on page 17. Bake as directed above or until pie is bubbling and golden.

VARIATION
PEACH BLUEBERRY CRUMB PIE

Prepare the same recipe as above, but use an unbaked pie shell and cover with Crumb Topping: In a small bowl combine ½ cup unsalted (sweet) butter, cut into bits, ½ cup light brown sugar, 1 cup flour, ½ teaspoon cinnamon, ¼ cup ground walnuts, and ½ teaspoon grated lemon rind. Mix until crumbly, then sprinkle over top of pie and bake 10 minutes at 450°F, and 25 minutes at 350°F, or until pie bubbles and topping is brown.

FRESH PEACH PIE

The best of midsummer peaches in a pie.
Pour some heavy cream over each
slice for peaches and cream.
This can be made with
fresh nectarines, too.

PREHEAT OVEN: 500°F.

PASTRY NEEDED: Unbaked 9-inch double-crust pie.

BAKING TIME: 5 minutes at 500°F, 25 minutes at 375°F.

SERVINGS: 6 to 8.

5 cups peeled, sliced fresh
   peaches (or nectarines)
⅓ cup sugar
2 tablespoons sugar
2 tablespoons unsalted (sweet)
   butter, cut into bits
½ teaspoon ground cinnamon
¼ teaspoon nutmeg

Mix all ingredients together until well blended. Pour into pastry shell, cap, and finish as described on pages 17-18. Bake as directed above or until pie is golden.

Peach Blueberry Pie prepared with
Mom's Flaky pastry and a lattice top.
A tempting end to a summer meal.

SOUR CHERRY PIE

*The color is perfect. I always
use a lattice top so that the bright
red bubbles through.*

PREHEAT OVEN: 425°F.

PASTRY NEEDED: Unbaked 9-inch
double-crust pie.

BAKING TIME: 10 minutes at 425°F,
30 minutes at 375°F.

SERVINGS: 6 to 8.

4 **cups pitted sour cherries**
1 **cup sugar**
2 **tablespoons flour**
2 **tablespoons unsalted (sweet)
   butter, cut into bits**
½ **teaspoon grated lemon rind**

Mix all ingredients together in a
medium-size mixing bowl. Pour into
pie shell and finish with lattice top
as described on page 17. Bake as
directed above.

PEACH CRUMB PIE

*This recipe probably originated
in the South because of its lavish use
of pecans. You can substitute
walnuts if you wish, also nectarines
in place of peaches.*

PREHEAT OVEN: 400°F.

PASTRY NEEDED: Unbaked 9-inch
pie shell.

BAKING TIME: 10 minutes at 400°F,
30 minutes at 350°F.

SERVINGS: 6 to 8.

½ **cup light brown sugar**
½ **cup flour**
1 **cup chopped pecans**
5 **tablespoons unsalted (sweet)
   butter, cut into bits**
5 **cups peeled and sliced fresh
   peaches (or nectarines)**
1 **tablespoon lemon juice**
⅓ **cup granulated sugar**
2 **tablespoons flour**

Mix together until crumbly the brown
sugar, ½ cup flour, nuts, and butter.
Sprinkle about one third of mixture
on bottom of pie shell. Combine
peaches, lemon juice, granulated
sugar, and 2 tablespoons flour. Pour
into pie shell, then top with remaining crumb mixture. Bake as directed
above or until pie is bubbling.

PRALINE PEACH PIE

*A very rich pie that I often
top with a scoop of peach ice cream,
for there's never too much of a good thing.*

PREHEAT OVEN: 375°F.

PASTRY NEEDED: Unbaked 9-inch
pie shell.

BAKING TIME: 10 minutes at 375°F,
40 minutes at 325°F.

SERVINGS: 6 to 8.

3 **eggs**
½ **cup heavy cream**
1 **cup dark corn syrup**
1 **teaspoon vanilla**
¾ **cup sugar**
3 **tablespoons flour**
1½ **cups peeled, pitted and
   chopped fresh peaches (or
   nectarines)**
1 **cup chopped pecans**

Beat the eggs, heavy cream, and corn
syrup together at medium speed of
electric mixer. Add vanilla, sugar, and
flour, beating until well blended. Fold
in peaches and pecans and pour into
pie shell. Bake as directed above or
until pie is set.

BERRY CRUMB PIE

Another way to enjoy fresh berries—wild or domestic. The amount of sugar used is determined by taste and by berry.

PREHEAT OVEN: 350°F.

PASTRY NEEDED: Baked 9-inch pie shell.

BAKING TIME: 15 minutes at 350°F.

SERVINGS: 6 to 8.

4 **cups fresh berries (blueberries, blackberries, strawberries, raspberries, boysenberries, dewberries, elderberries, or gooseberries)**

¾ **cup sugar (more or less, depending on berry used)**

3 **tablespoons cornstarch**

¼ **cup orange juice**

½ **teaspoon grated lemon rind**

½ **cup unsalted (sweet) butter, cut into bits**

½ **cup sugar**

1 **cup flour**

¼ **cup nuts, ground**
   Dash nutmeg

Place the berries, ¾ cup sugar, cornstarch, orange juice, and lemon rind in a heavy saucepan over medium heat. Bring to boil, lower heat, and cook until juice thickens. Set aside. In medium-size mixing bowl combine the butter, ½ cup sugar, flour, nuts, and nutmeg with your fingers until crumbly mixture has been achieved. Pour berry mixture into pie shell and cover with crumb topping. Bake as directed above or until crumb topping has set and browned slightly. Let cool before serving.

FRESH PEAR PIE

A terrific way to enjoy Bosc or Bartlett pears. If the pears are not too ripe, this is almost indistinguishable from apple pie.

PREHEAT OVEN: 450°F.

PASTRY NEEDED: Unbaked 9-inch double-crust pie.

BAKING TIME: 10 minutes at 450°F, 30 minutes at 350°F.

SERVINGS: 6 to 8.

5 **cups peeled, cored, and sliced fresh pears**

2 **tablespoons flour**

⅓ **cup sugar**

1 **tablespoon lemon juice**

1 **teaspoon grated lemon rind**

½ **teaspoon ground cinnamon**

¼ **teaspoon ground nutmeg**

3 **tablespoons unsalted (sweet) butter, cut into bits**

Mix all ingredients together until well blended. Put in pie shell, and finish with either closed top or lattice top, as described on page 17. Bake as directed above or until golden.

FRENCH PEAR PIE

An open-faced pie that is more like a tart.
It should be eaten soon after baking
as pears often darken as they sit.
Serve with slightly sweetened whipped cream.

PREHEAT OVEN: 400°F.
PASTRY NEEDED: Unbaked 9-inch
pie shell.
BAKING TIME: 10 minutes at 400°F,
30 minutes at 350°F.
SERVINGS: 6 to 8.

4 cups peeled, cored, and sliced
   pears
1 tablespoon lemon juice
½ teaspoon ground nutmeg
½ teaspoon grated orange rind
¼ cup unsalted (sweet) butter,
   melted
½ cup brown sugar
½ cup granulated sugar
½ cup flour
3 eggs
   Confectioners' sugar

Mix the pear slices with lemon juice,
nutmeg, and orange rind. Arrange in
pie shell. Mix butter, sugars, flour, and
eggs together and pour on top of
pears. Bake as directed above or until
custard is set. Sprinkle top with confectioners' sugar while still warm and
serve immediately.

Luscious French Pear Pie
in a Sweet Pastry Crust.
A sophisticated dessert.

GINGER PEAR PIE

I love the zest ginger adds to fresh,
crunchy Bosc pears. Serve with a thin
slice of Parmesan cheese for an
extra-special treat.

PREHEAT OVEN: 450°F.
PASTRY NEEDED: Unbaked 9-inch
double-crust pie.
BAKING TIME: 10 minutes at 450°F,
30 minutes at 350°F.
SERVINGS: 6 to 8.

5 cups peeled, cored and cut up
   fresh winter pears (cut into
   chunks)
½ cup sugar
1 tablespoon grated orange rind
¼ cup orange juice
¼ cup flour
½ teaspoon ground cinnamon
¼ teaspoon ground ginger
¼ cup ground nutmeg
¼ cup unsalted (sweet) butter, cut
   into bits
¼ cup diced candied ginger
   (optional)

Mix all ingredients together until well
blended. Put in pie shell, cap, and
finish as described on pages 17-18.
Bake as directed above or until golden.

CRANBERRY NUT PIE

A great fall dessert that can be
enjoyed all year round if you, as I do,
keep cranberries in your freezer.
A scoop of vanilla ice cream is best
on a warm slice of this colorful pie,
which lends itself to fancy tops.

PREHEAT OVEN: 450°F.
PASTRY NEEDED: Unbaked 9-inch
double-crust pie.
BAKING TIME: 10 minutes at 450°F,
30 minutes at 375°F.
SERVINGS: 6 to 8.

4 cups fresh cranberries
1 teaspoon grated lemon rind
1½ cups whole walnut pieces
2 tablespoons unsalted (sweet)
   butter, cut into bits
1 cup light brown sugar
¼ cup flour
   Dash of cinnamon

Mix all ingredients together until well
blended. Pour into pastry shell, cap,
and finish as described on pages 17-18.
Bake as directed above or until golden.

CRANBERRY RAISIN PIE

The sweetness of the raisins is a wonderful counter to the tartness of cranberries. Whipped cream or ice cream adds a nice touch to the finished pie.

PREHEAT OVEN: 450°F.

PASTRY NEEDED: Unbaked 9-inch double-crust pie.

BAKING TIME: 10 minutes at 450°F, 30 minutes at 375°F.

SERVINGS: 6 to 8.

  3 cups chopped fresh cranberries
1½ cups seedless raisins
  1 cup sugar (or to taste)
  ½ cup flour
  1 teaspoon cinnamon
  2 tablespoons unsalted (sweet) butter, cut into bits

Mix all ingredients together until well blended. Pour into pastry shell, cap, and finish as described on pages 17-18. Bake as directed above or until golden.

PLUM PIE

Italian prune plums are perfect for pies and make a fine substitution for peaches in Peach Custard or Peach Crumb Pie. Serve this warm with unsweetened heavy cream poured over the top.

PREHEAT OVEN: 450°F.

PASTRY NEEDED: Unbaked 9-inch double-crust pie.

BAKING TIME: 10 minutes at 450°F, 30 minutes at 350°F.

SERVINGS: 6 to 8.

  4 cups pitted, quartered prune plums
  ½ cup sugar
  ¼ cup flour
  ¼ teaspoon ground nutmeg
  1 tablespoon orange juice
  1 teaspoon grated orange rind
  2 tablespoons unsalted (sweet) butter, cut into bits
Confectioners' sugar

Mix together all ingredients except confectioners' sugar and put in pie shell. Finish with lattice top as described on page 17. Bake as directed above or until pie bubbles and pastry is golden. Sprinkle with confectioners' sugar while still warm and serve immediately.

OLD-FASHIONED RAISIN PIE

Raisin pies are an old-time favorite. They are easy to make and call for ingredients one generally has on hand.

PREHEAT OVEN: 450°F.

PASTRY NEEDED: Unbaked 9-inch double-crust pie.

BAKING TIME: 10 minutes at 450°F, 30 minutes at 350°F.

SERVINGS: 6 to 8.

  2 cups dark seedless raisins
1½ cups water
  ½ cup orange juice
  1 cup sugar
  3 egg yolks
  2 tablespoons flour
  2 tablespoons vinegar
  1 teaspoon grated orange rind
  3 tablespoons unsalted (sweet) butter, cut into bits

Simmer the raisins in water and orange juice for about 5 minutes. Remove from heat. Stir in remaining ingredients, pour into pie shell, and finish with lattice top as described on page 17. Bake as directed above or until pie is bubbling and golden.

RUM RAISIN PIE

A terrific holiday pie. Serve warm with rum raisin or coffee ice cream, or a dollop of sour cream.

PREHEAT OVEN: 450°F.

PASTRY NEEDED: Unbaked 9-inch double-crust pie.

BAKING TIME: 10 minutes at 450°F, 30 minutes at 350°F.

SERVINGS: 6 to 8.

2 cups dark seedless raisins
  Hot water
2 eggs
½ cup sugar
1 tablespoon cornstarch
¾ cup cranapple juice
¼ cup dark rum
1 tablespoon cinnamon
  Confectioners' sugar

Cover raisins and apples with hot water and let sit for about ten minutes. Drain and combine with remaining ingredients except confectioners' sugar. Pour into pie shell, and finish with lattice top as described on page 17. Bake as directed above or until pie is bubbling and pastry is golden. Sprinkle top with confectioners' sugar while still warm and serve.

SOUR CREAM RAISIN PIE

A New England favorite—the maple flavor blends beautifully with the dried fruit and nuts. Serve with a dollop of sour cream drizzled with maple syrup.

PREHEAT OVEN: 400°F.

PASTRY NEEDED: Unbaked 9-inch pie shell.

BAKING TIME: 10 minutes at 400°F, 40 minutes at 350°F.

SERVINGS: 6 to 8.

2 cups raisins
  Hot water
3 eggs, beaten
¾ cup maple syrup
1 tablespoon lemon juice
1 cup sour cream
¾ cup chopped walnuts

Soak raisins, covered with hot water, for 5 minutes. Drain well, then mix with rest of ingredients except walnuts. Pour into pie shell, sprinkle walnuts on top, and bake as directed above or until pie is well set.

RHUBARB PIE

Fresh rhubarb pie is the harbinger of summer. I love its tartness and color. Vanilla ice cream is the perfect topping.

PREHEAT OVEN: 450°F.

PASTRY NEEDED: Unbaked 9-inch double-crust pie.

BAKING TIME: 10 minutes at 450°F, 35 minutes at 350°F.

SERVINGS: 6 to 8.

5 cups diced fresh rhubarb
⅓ cup flour
1 cup sugar (for young, tender stalks; older stalks may require more)
1 teaspoon orange juice
2 tablespoons unsalted (sweet) butter, cut into bits
1 tablespoon grated orange rind

Mix all ingredients together and put in pie shell. Finish with lattice top as described on page 17. Bake as directed above or until pie bubbles and pastry is golden.

RHUBARB STRAWBERRY PIE

My oldest son's favorite pie. I don't know whether it's the taste or the fact that strawberries and rhubarb are ripe for pie-making when school is about ready to be out.

PREHEAT OVEN: 450°F.

PASTRY NEEDED: Unbaked 9-inch double-crust pie.

BAKING TIME: 10 minutes at 450°F, 30 minutes at 375°F.

SERVINGS: 6 to 8.

2 cups diced fresh rhubarb
2½ to 3 cups whole hulled strawberries
1 cup sugar
¼ cup flour
3 tablespoons unsalted (sweet) butter, cut into bits
¼ teaspoon ground nutmeg
Confectioners' sugar or cinnamon sugar mixture

Mix together all but last ingredient and put into pie shell. Finish with lattice top as described on page 17. Bake as directed above or until pie bubbles and pastry is golden. Sprinkle top with confectioners' sugar or a mixture of cinnamon and sugar while pie is still warm.

CHIFFON, CHEESE, CUSTARD, AND CREAM

COFFEE CHIFFON PIE

This makes an easy, unexpected-dinner-guest dessert.

PASTRY NEEDED: Baked 9-inch pie shell, either traditional pastry or crumb crust.

SERVINGS: 6 to 8.

1 envelope unflavored gelatin
¼ cup cold water
½ cup superfine sugar
4 tablespoons fine instant coffee powder
2 cups heavy cream
2 tablespoons freeze-dried instant coffee granules

Dissolve unflavored gelatin in cold water. Heat briefly if necessary to dissolve. Set aside. Mix together the sugar and fine instant coffee powder. Whip the heavy cream until it holds firm peaks, then stir in the coffee-powder mixture and dissolved gelatin. Pour into prepared pie shell, sprinkle top with freeze-dried instant coffee granules, and refrigerate until firm.

PUMPKIN CHIFFON PIE

A terrific ending to a big holiday meal as it is lighter than the traditional pumpkin pie.

PASTRY NEEDED: Baked 9-inch Gingersnap Crumb Crust (page 25).

SERVINGS: 6 to 8.

1 envelope unflavored gelatin
1 tablespoon water
2 cups pureed cooked pumpkin
½ cup granulated sugar
4 egg yolks, lightly beaten
½ cup heavy cream
½ teaspoon ground ginger
½ teaspoon ground cinnamon
¼ teaspoon ground nutmeg
3 egg whites
¼ cup granulated sugar
½ cup heavy cream
1 teaspoon confectioners' sugar

Dissolve gelatin in water. Combine pumpkin and ½ cup granulated sugar, then stir in softened gelatin. Add the egg yolks, ½ cup heavy cream, and spices and cook until thick. Remove from heat and cool slightly. Beat egg whites with ¼ cup granulated sugar until stiff and fold into pumpkin mixture. Pour into prepared crumb crust and chill until set. Whip ½ cup heavy cream with confectioners' sugar and pipe rosettes across top of pie. Refrigerate until ready to serve.

GRAPEFRUIT CHIFFON PIE

A delicious yet light dessert that does not make you feel too guilty when you go off your diet.

PASTRY NEEDED: Baked 9-inch crumb crust.

SERVINGS: 8.

1 envelope unflavored gelatin
1¾ cups fresh grapefruit juice
1 cup sugar
1 teaspoon grated grapefruit rind
3 egg yolks
3 egg whites, beaten into stiff peaks
½ cup heavy cream, whipped
8 grapefruit sections, membrane and seeds removed

Dissolve gelatin in grapefruit juice in a saucepan. Add sugar and grated grapefruit rind and cook until well blended. Whisk a little of the grapefruit juice mixture into the egg yolks, then pour into the saucepan with remaining grapefruit mixture. Cook for a few minutes until mixture begins to coat a spoon. Remove from heat, cool a bit, and alternately add beaten egg whites and whipped cream. Pour into prepared crumb crust, chill at least 3 hours or until well set, and decorate by placing 1 grapefruit section on each slice of pie. Serve immediately.

CHOCOLATE CHIFFON PIE

Chocolate chiffon filling covered with whipped cream and drizzled with chocolate syrup.

PASTRY NEEDED: Baked 9-inch pie shell or crumb crusts.

SERVINGS: 6 to 8.

1 envelope unflavored gelatin
¼ cup granulated sugar
1 cup half-and-half
3 squares unsweetened chocolate
4 egg yolks, lightly beaten
1 teaspoon vanilla
4 egg whites
½ cup granulated sugar
1 cup heavy cream
2 tablespoons confectioners' sugar
1 tablespoon chocolate syrup

Combine unflavored gelatin and ¼ cup granulated sugar in top of double boiler. Add the half-and-half and chocolate and stir constantly over simmering water until chocolate melts. Then beat with a hand beater until well blended. Mix a couple of tablespoons of the warm chocolate mixture with the egg yolks and vanilla. Stir quickly to blend and pour this into remaining chocolate mixture, beating constantly. Cook, still beating, until chocolate mixture has thickened. Remove from heat and cool.

Beat egg whites with ½ cup granulated sugar until stiff, then fold into the chocolate mixture and pour into prepared pie shell. Refrigerate until firm.

Whip the heavy cream with confectioners' sugar and spread over top of chilled pie. Or if desired, put into a pastry tube and make rosettes on top. Drizzle with chocolate syrup and refrigerate until ready to serve.

BERRY CHIFFON PIE

For a fancy touch, put some whipped cream in a pastry tube and decorate the top of the pie, adding a few whole berries to the design.

PASTRY NEEDED: Baked 9-inch pie shell or any of the crumb crusts.

SERVINGS: 4 to 6.

1 **envelope unflavored gelatin**
2 **tablespoons cool water**
¼ **cup boiling water**
1 **cup sugar**
1 **cup mashed berries (any kind)**
1 **cup heavy cream**
2 **egg whites**
1 **tablespoon sugar**
1 **cup whole berries**

In a mixing bowl, dissolve the gelatin in 2 tablespoons cool water. Add ¼ cup boiling water and stir. Mix in 1 cup sugar and 1 cup mashed berries. Let set until it begins to firm.

Whip 1 cup heavy cream and set aside. In separate bowl whip egg whites with 1 tablespoon sugar until stiff but not dry. Add whipped cream and egg whites alternately to the gelatin-berry mixture. Fold in the whole berries and pour into prepared pie shell. Refrigerate for at least 1 hour before serving.

Berry Chiffon Pie in a Graham Cracker Crust, baked in a heart-shaped pan and topped with whipped cream and fresh raspberries.

LEMON CHIFFON PIE

Lime, orange, or tangerine juice can be used instead of lemon but adjust the amount of sugar added. Always refreshing, a light chiffon pie is achieved by having the gelatin mixture just firm when adding the whipped egg whites and cream.

PASTRY NEEDED: Baked 9-inch pie shell, either traditional pastry or crumb crust.

SERVINGS: 6 to 8.

1 **envelope unflavored gelatin**
⅓ **cup lemon juice (or ⅔ cup lime juice or 1 cup orange or tangerine juice)**
½ **cup sugar (less 2 tablespoons for orange or tangerine)**
4 **egg yolks**
1 **teaspoon grated lemon rind**
4 **egg whites, beaten stiff with 2 tablespoons superfine sugar**
½ **cup heavy cream, whipped with 2 tablespoons confectioners' sugar**
  Lemon slices, with the edges brushed with egg whites and dipped in sugar, for garnish (optional)

Dissolve gelatin in the juice. Add sugar, beat in egg yolks and rind, and chill until just firm. Then alternately add beaten egg whites and whipped cream to the fruit juice mixture, folding gently as you go. Pour into prepared pie shell, garnish top with lemon slices, and serve immediately or keep refrigerated until ready to serve.

SAINT THOMAS PIE

PASTRY NEEDED: Baked 9-inch crumb crust.
SERVINGS: 6 to 8.

¾ cup grated fresh coconut, toasted
1 envelope unflavored gelatin
½ cup fresh lime juice
6 egg yolks
½ cup granulated sugar
4 tablespoons light rum
1 tablespoon grated lime rind
4 egg whites, beaten stiff with ¼ cup granulated sugar
1 cup heavy cream, whipped with 2 tablespoons confectioners' sugar
1 lime, thinly sliced for garnish

Put ½ cup of toasted coconut in bottom of prepared crumb crust. Dissolve gelatin in lime juice. In saucepan, beat egg yolks and ½ cup granulated sugar until thick. Add dissolved gelatin and cook over medium heat until mixture thickens and coats a spoon. Remove from heat and cool slightly. Add rum and grated lime rind. Stir in half of the beaten egg whites, then alternately add remaining whites and whipped cream to create a light marbleized effect. Mound in crumb crust, sprinkle with remaining toasted coconut, and decorate with lime slices.

KIWI PIE

When I spoke of kiwi pie to friends visiting from Australia they couldn't believe that I would eat a kiwi, which to them is a native bird. Kiwis as I know them are called Chinese Gooseberries Down Under. Whatever the name, they are a wonderful, refreshing fruit.

PASTRY NEEDED: Baked 9-inch Nut Crust (page 25.)
SERVINGS: 6 to 8.

1 envelope unflavored gelatin
¼ cup cold water
2 cups peeled, sliced kiwis
1 teaspoon grated lime rind
3 tablespoons lime juice
¼ cup sugar
3 egg whites, beaten until stiff
½ cup heavy cream, whipped

Dissolve gelatin in cold water and mix with 1½ cups kiwis, lime rind, lime juice, and sugar. Chill to thicken. When well chilled, mix in alternately the beaten egg whites and the whipped cream. Pour into prepared pie shell, decorate top with remaining ½ cup kiwis, chill until firm, and serve immediately.

HONEY CHEESE PIE

This pie is based on a Greek dessert. Don't be alarmed if the surface of the pie cracks—this happens sometimes but doesn't harm the taste.

PREHEAT OVEN: 425°F
PASTRY NEEDED: Unbaked 9-inch pie shell.
BAKING TIME: 10 minutes at 425°F, 45 minutes at 325°F.
SERVINGS: 6 to 8.

2 cups pot or farmer cheese (or cottage cheese)
¾ cup honey
4 eggs
1 tablespoon grated lemon rind
½ teaspoon cinnamon

With electric mixer, beat the cheese until it is smooth. Whip in the honey and add the eggs 1 at a time, blending after each. Beat in the lemon rind and cinnamon. Pour into pie shell and bake as directed above. Cool before serving.

CREAM CHEESE PIE

Turn this into a party-perfect pie by topping with sour cream and a spoonful of preserves or fresh fruit.

PASTRY NEEDED: Baked 9-inch crumb crust.

SERVINGS: 6 to 8.

1 **cup cream cheese**
1 **cup cottage cheese**
½ **cup heavy cream**
1½ **cups sweetened condensed milk**
½ **teaspoon lemon juice**

Place the cream cheese and cottage cheese in small bowl of electric mixer. Whip until well blended. Add the heavy cream, sweetened condensed milk, and lemon juice and beat to mix. Pour into prepared crumb crust and refrigerate for about 3 hours before serving.

CHERRY CHEESE PIE

Use canned cherries for this dessert when fresh are not available. It's always pretty to look at and delicious to eat.

PASTRY NEEDED: Baked 9-inch crumb crust.

SERVINGS: 6 to 8.

1 **cup cream cheese, softened**
¼ **cup sour cream**
½ **teaspoon grated lemon rind**
2 **cups pitted Bing cherries**
½ **cup sugar**
2 **tablespoons lemon juice**
1 **cup water**
3 **tablespoons cornstarch**

Whip the cream cheese, sour cream, and lemon rind together at medium speed of electric mixer. Pour into prepared crumb crust and refrigerate, covered with wax paper.

Combine Bing cherries, sugar, lemon juice, and water in heavy saucepan and bring just to a boil over medium heat. Remove from heat, drain liquid from cherries, and set cherries aside. Measure 1¼ cups liquid into medium-size saucepan. Blend in cornstarch and bring to boil over medium heat, stirring constantly until liquid has thickened. Remove from heat. Stir in drained cherries and mix to blend. Cool thoroughly, then pour over chilled cheese-filled crumb crust. Return to refrigerator for about 1 hour or until pie is well set.

ORANGE CHEESE PIE

An easy-to-make, cheese-cake-like pie that gets better as it "ages." Bake it a day or so in advance and refrigerate until ready to serve.

PASTRY NEEDED: Baked 9-inch crumb crust.

SERVINGS: 6 to 8.

1½ **cups ricotta cheese**
½ **cup sour cream**
½ **cup granulated sugar**
3 **egg yolks**
1 **tablespoon Grand Marnier**
1½ **tablespoons grated orange rind**
1 **cup orange segments, membranes removed**
1 **cup semi-sweet chocolate bits**
3 **egg whites, beaten stiff with 4 tablespoons superfine sugar**
Orange slices and chocolate shavings for garnish

Beat cheese, sour cream, granulated sugar, and egg yolks together at medium speed with electric mixer. Add Grand Marnier and orange rind and beat until well blended. Fold in orange segments and chocolate bits and then the beaten egg whites. Pour into prepared crumb crust, garnish with chocolate shavings and orange slices, and refrigerate until ready to serve.

CHOCOLATE CHEESE PIE

A cinch to make and a family favorite.

PASTRY NEEDED: Baked 9-inch crumb crust.

SERVINGS: 6 to 8.

3 squares unsweetened chocolate, melted
1 pound cream cheese, softened
1 egg yolk
1½ cups sweetened condensed milk
1 tablespoon grated orange rind
1 cup heavy cream
2 tablespoons confectioners' sugar
1 teaspoon fresh grated orange rind

Combine melted chocolate, cream cheese, egg yolk, sweetened condensed milk, and orange rind in medium-size bowl and beat until well blended. Pour into prepared crumb crust and refrigerate for 2 hours.

Whip heavy cream with confectioners' sugar and spread on top of the chilled pie. Sprinkle whipped cream with fresh grated orange rind and refrigerate until ready to serve.

Chocolate Cheese Pie, here with the topping applied in a spiral.

BERRY CREAM CHEESE PIE

PASTRY NEEDED: Baked 9-inch crumb crust.

SERVINGS: 6 to 8.

1 cup cream cheese, softened
¼ cup superfine sugar
1 teaspoon vanilla
1 cup heavy cream
3 cups fresh berries

In mixing bowl combine cream cheese, sugar, and vanilla until well blended. Whip in heavy cream and turn into prepared crumb crust. Smooth top, cover with fresh berries, and refrigerate until serving time.

CUSTARD PIE

One of my favorites. To prevent a soggy crust you can partially bake (or blind bake) your shell for about 5 minutes before pouring in the custard filling. You will sometimes see a recipe telling you to bake the custard in a pie plate the exact size of your pie shell and then slip it into the baked pastry. Try it if you like, but all I ever achieve is an empty baked pie shell and a messy batch of custard.

PREHEAT OVEN: 450°F.

PASTRY NEEDED: Partially baked (blind-baked) 9-inch pie shell.

BAKING TIME: 10 minutes at 450°F, 30 minutes at 300°F.

SERVINGS: 6 to 8.

4 eggs
1 cup milk
½ cup heavy cream
¼ cup sugar (or to taste)
1 tablespoon unsalted (sweet) butter, cut into bits
½ teaspoon vanilla
¼ teaspoon nutmeg

Beat the eggs, milk, and cream together. Add the sugar and stir until dissolved. Add the butter, vanilla, and nutmeg and blend well. Pour into prepared pie shell and bake as directed above or until custard is set. Remove from oven and cool at least 45 minutes before serving.

CHOCOLATE CHESS PIE

This is my best-known dessert. People always ask for the recipe which, until now, has been my secret. This is the richest dessert you can offer. A tiny sliver topped with slightly sweetened whipped cream will ensure your reputation as a terrific cook. It is a plain pie that makes up in taste what it lacks in looks.

PREHEAT OVEN: 350°F.
PASTRY NEEDED: Unbaked 9-inch pie shell.
BAKING TIME: 35 minutes.
SERVINGS: At least 10, since it is best served in small slices, but those with a sweet tooth can ask for seconds.

- 1 **cup sugar**
- 1 **tablespoon flour**
- ⅓ **cup unsweetened cocoa**
- 2 **egg yolks**
- 1 **whole egg**
- 3 **tablespoons water**
- 1 **teaspoon white vinegar**
- ½ **cup unsalted (sweet) butter, melted and cooled**

Combine sugar, flour, and cocoa in a bowl and set aside. Beat egg yolks and whole egg with electric mixer until well blended. Add water and vinegar and beat until frothy. Pour in cooled, melted butter and blend at low speed. Slowly add cocoa mixture and beat until thoroughly mixed. Pour into pie shell and bake as directed above.

VARIATIONS

LEMON OR ORANGE CHESS PIE

Eliminate cocoa and add 1 tablespoon white cornmeal and 1 tablespoon grated rind of lemon and orange. Replace water with equal amounts of lemon and orange juice.

PIÑA COLADA CHESS PIE

Eliminate cocoa and add 1 additional tablespoon flour, ¼ cup coconut cream, and 1 cup crushed pineapple. Replace 2 tablespoons of the water with 2 tablespoons rum.

PINEAPPLE CHESS PIE

Eliminate cocoa. Replace water and vinegar with 4 tablespoons pineapple juice. Add 1½ cups canned crushed pineapple, well drained, or fresh if you can get it.

SOUR CREAM CHESS PIE

Eliminate cocoa. Add 1 cup sour cream and 1 tablespoon white cornmeal.

AUNTIE BLOSSOM'S SWEET POTATO PIE

Sweet Potato Pie can be served as a dessert, a side dish, or a part of breakfast.

PREHEAT OVEN: 425°F.
PASTRY NEEDED: Unbaked 9-inch traditional or whole wheat pie shell.
BAKING TIME: 15 minutes at 425°F, 40 minutes at 350°F.
SERVINGS: 6 to 8.

- 2 **cups mashed cooked sweet potato**
- ½ **cup unsalted (sweet) butter, softened**
- 3 **eggs**
- 1 **cup milk**
- 1 **cup sugar**
- ¼ **teaspoon nutmeg**
- 1 **teaspoon vanilla**
- ¼ **cup bourbon (or orange juice)**

Mix all ingredients together, beating until well blended. Pour into pie shell, and bake as directed above or until pie is set. Lower heat if crust starts browning too quickly.

CARROT PIE

One of my favorite fall pies, lighter than sweet potato or pumpkin, but similar in taste and texture. A spoonful of whipped cream adds an extra touch to each serving.

PREHEAT OVEN: 450°F.

PASTRY NEEDED: Unbaked 9-inch traditional or whole wheat pie shell.

BAKING TIME: 5 minutes at 450°F, 45 minutes at 325°F.

SERVINGS: 6 to 8.

    2 cups pureed cooked carrots
 1½ cups evaporated milk
    ½ cup sugar
    2 eggs
    1 teaspoon cinnamon
    ¼ teaspoon ginger
    ¼ teaspoon nutmeg

Mix all ingredients together at medium speed of electric mixer, blending thoroughly. Pour into pie shell and bake as directed above or until pie is set. Let cool about 10 minutes before serving.

BUTTERMILK PIE

Just a few ingredients combine to make a divine dessert.

PREHEAT OVEN: 450°F.

PASTRY NEEDED: Unbaked 9-inch pie shell.

BAKING TIME: 10 minutes at 450°F, 30 to 40 minutes at 325°F.

SERVINGS: 6 to 8.

    ½ cup unsalted (sweet) butter, melted and cooled
    1 cup sugar
    ½ cup flour
    3 eggs
 1½ cups buttermilk
    1 teaspoon vanilla

Beat all ingredients together in medium-size mixing bowl. Pour into pie shell and bake as directed above. Let set about 10 minutes before cutting.

SQUASH PIE

Developed, I'm certain, after a bountiful winter squash harvest. Lessen the sugar and you can use this pie as a side dish.

PREHEAT OVEN: 400°F.

PASTRY NEEDED: Unbaked 9-inch traditional or whole wheat pie shell.

BAKING TIME: 10 minutes at 400°F, 30 minutes at 350°F.

SERVINGS: 6 to 8.

    2 cups pureed cooked fresh squash (butternut, acorn, Hubbard, or other fleshy winter squash)
    ¾ cup sugar plus ¼ cup maple sugar or syrup (or just 1 cup sugar)
    3 eggs
    1 cup milk
    ½ cup heavy cream
    1 tablespoon unsalted (sweet) butter, melted
    1 teaspoon cinnamon
    ¼ teaspoon ginger

Mix all ingredients together until well blended and pour into pie shell. Bake as directed above or until pie is set. Lower heat if crust starts browning too fast.

PUMPKIN PIE

I try to use fresh pumpkin during the fall, but since it is a family favorite, I frequently use canned pumpkin when fresh is not available. If you do use fresh add an additional egg.

PREHEAT OVEN: 400°F.
PASTRY NEEDED: Unbaked 9-inch shell.
BAKING TIME: 45 minutes at 400°F.
SERVINGS: 6 to 8.

  2 cups pureed cooked pumpkin
  ½ cup sugar
  2 eggs
  1 cup evaporated milk
  1 teaspoon ground cinnamon
  ¼ teaspoon ginger
    Dash each of ground cloves and nutmeg

Mix all ingredients together until well blended. Pour into pie shell and bake as directed above or until pie is well set. (Pumpkin pies frequently bubble on top and turn dark as they bake; if bubbles form, break them with the tines of a fork. Lower heat if pie begins to brown too fast.)

PEACH CUSTARD PIE

Peaches and cream in a pastry shell. Quick and easy and so delicious.

PREHEAT OVEN: 400°F.
PASTRY NEEDED: Unbaked 9-inch pie shell.
BAKING TIME: 10 minutes at 400°F, 20 minutes at 325°F.
SERVINGS: 6 to 8.

  3 pounds peaches (or nectarines), peeled, halved, and pitted
  ⅔ cup granulated sugar
  ⅓ cup light brown sugar
  2 tablespoons flour
  1 cup heavy cream
  1 tablespoon cinnamon/sugar mixture (¾ cup sugar to 3 teaspoons cinnamon)

Place the peaches cut-side down in pie shell until it is well filled. Mix the sugars and flour together and sprinkle over the peaches. Pour heavy cream over top, sprinkle with cinnamon/sugar mixture and bake as directed above or until set.

COCONUT CUSTARD PIE

An all-time favorite. Again, it is best made with fresh coconut but you can always substitute prepared.

PREHEAT OVEN: 400°F.
PASTRY NEEDED: Unbaked 9-inch pie shell.
BAKING TIME: 30 to 35 minutes at 400°F.
SERVINGS: 6 to 8.

  3 eggs
  1 cup milk
  ½ cup heavy cream
  1 tablespoon unsalted (sweet) butter
  ½ teaspoon grated orange rind
  ½ cup sugar
  ¾ cup plus 3 tablespoons grated fresh coconut

On medium speed of electric mixer beat the eggs. Add milk and heavy cream and beat to blend. Add butter, orange rind, sugar, and ¾ cup coconut, mixing until blended. Pour into pie shell, sprinkle with 3 tablespoons grated coconut, and bake as directed above or until custard is well set. Cool before serving.

Tropical Coconut Custard Pie prepared with Mom's Flaky Pastry and garnished with freshly grated coconut.

NESSELRODE PIE

It took me a long time to find a recipe that worked for a pie I had always heard about but had never tasted. It reminds me of an Italian dessert called cannoli and is perhaps based on the filling for it.

PASTRY NEEDED: Baked 9-inch traditional pie shell or any crumb crust.

SERVINGS: 6 to 8.

- 1 **envelope unflavored gelatin**
- 4 **tablespoons light rum**
- 2 **cups warm milk**
- 2 **egg yolks**
- 2 **tablespoons granulated sugar**
- 2 **egg whites, whipped stiff with ¼ cup superfine sugar**
- ½ **cup semi-sweet chocolate bits**
- 1 **cup prepared Nesselrode fruits (Rafetto is the brand I use) or 1 cup chopped glazed fruit**
- 2 **tablespoons semi-sweet chocolate shavings for garnish**

Dissolve gelatin in rum in a saucepan. Add the warm milk, egg yolks, and granulated sugar. Cook until mixture thickens and coats a spoon. Remove from heat and cool. Fold in beaten egg whites, chocolate bits, and fruit. Pour into prepared pie shell and chill until well set. Sprinkle chocolate shavings on top before serving.

BUTTERSCOTCH PIE

Another flavor rarely made from scratch but so much better when it is. Topped with whipped cream or meringue.

PASTRY NEEDED: Baked 9-inch traditional pie shell or any crumb crust.

SERVINGS: 6 to 8.

- ½ **cup unsalted (sweet) butter**
- 1 **cup light brown sugar**
- ½ **teaspoon instant coffee powder**
- 1 **cup boiling water**
- 3 **tablespoons flour**
- 2 **tablespoons cornstarch**
- 1½ **cups milk**
- 3 **egg yolks**
  Aunt Frances' Never-Fail Meringue, page 27, or Whipped Cream Topping, page 26.

Melt the butter in heavy frying pan over very low heat. Add sugar and coffee and stir to mix. Bring to a boil, stirring constantly, until mixture turns a very golden-brown color. Whisk in boiling water and stir to blend well. Remove from heat and set aside.

Mix flour and cornstarch together in heavy saucepan. Whisk in milk and egg yolks and cook over medium heat, stirring constantly until mixture boils. Boil 1 minute and immediately remove from heat. Add coffee and butter mixture and stir to blend. Cool and pour into prepared pie shell.

If using meringue, follow procedure described on page 27 and bake at 350°F for 12 to 15 minutes or until the meringue is well browned. If using Whipped Cream Topping, refrigerate filled pie for at least 2 hours before adding topping.

VANILLA CREAM PIE

The most basic of pie fillings. For variety stir in fruit, chocolate bits, or any crunchy candy and top the pie with meringue or whipped cream.

PREHEAT OVEN: 400°F.

PASTRY NEEDED: Baked 9-inch traditional pie shell or crumb crust.

BAKING TIME: Meringue top, 10 minutes at 400°F.

SERVINGS: 6 to 8.

¾ cup sugar
2 tablespoons flour
2 tablespoons cornstarch
2 cups warm milk
3 egg yolks
1 tablespoon unsalted (sweet) butter, melted
1½ teaspoons vanilla
   Aunt Frances' Never-Fail Meringue, page 27

Mix sugar, flour, and cornstarch together in medium-size saucepan, then stir in warm milk. Beat some of the milk mixture into the egg yolks, then combine with contents of saucepan. Cook over medium heat until thickened. Stir in butter and vanilla and remove from heat. Pour into prepared pie shell, top with meringue, and bake according to the directions on page 27.

YOGURT PIE

A simple-to-make, absolutely delicious fresh fruit pie. My special favorite is blueberry but you can use any fruit you like.

PASTRY NEEDED: Baked 9-inch nut or crumb crust.

SERVINGS: 6 to 8.

1 13-ounce can sweetened condensed milk
8 ounces unflavored yogurt
1 large egg
¼ cup fresh lemon juice
1 teaspoon grated lemon or orange rind
2 cups fresh fruit, prepared for eating (peeled, seeded, hulled, etc.)

Combine all but last ingredient and beat until thick. Fold in fruit, pour into crumb crust, and chill until set. Serve immediately.

RHUBARB CUSTARD PIE

One of my Aunt Frances' pies. Topped with her never-fail meringue, this is a superb springtime dessert.

PREHEAT OVEN: 425°F.

PASTRY NEEDED: Unbaked 9-inch pie shell.

BAKING TIME: 10 minutes at 425°F, 30 minutes at 350°F.

SERVINGS: 6 to 8.

3 cups diced rhubarb
1½ cups sugar
2 tablespoons cornstarch
3 egg yolks
½ teaspoon ground nutmeg
   Aunt Frances' Never-Fail Meringue, page 27

Cover rhubarb with cold water and soak for 10 minutes. Drain well. Combine with sugar and cornstarch. Stir in the egg yolks, mix well, and pour into pie shell. Sprinkle with nutmeg and bake as directed above. Then remove from oven, cover with meringue, and bake as described on page 27.

KEY LIME PIE

Key limes can be found only in the Florida Keys or in the Caribbean. Once in a while I get a shipment from a friend who lives in the Bahamas, but generally I rely on the limes I get at the fruit market.

PREHEAT OVEN: 350°F.

PASTRY NEEDED: Baked 9-inch pie shell.

BAKING TIME: 15 minutes at 350°F.

SERVINGS: 6 to 8.

  5 **egg yolks**
  1 **cup canned sweetened condensed milk**
  ½ **cup fresh key lime juice**
  1 **tablespoon grated lime rind**
    Aunt Frances' Never-Fail Meringue, page 27, or Whipped Cream Topping, page 26

Beat the egg yolks until thick and creamy. Add the sweetened condensed milk and beat until well blended. Stir in the lime juice and rind, mixing thoroughly. Pour into prepared pie shell and bake as directed above. Remove from oven, top with meringue, and bake as described on page 27.

Or remove from oven, chill thoroughly, and cover with Whipped Cream Topping.

Tangy Key Lime Pie baked in Mom's Flaky Pastry and topped with Aunt Frances' Never-Fail Meringue. Use a cookie cutter to make the decorative trim.

AUNT FRANCES' LEMON MERINGUE PIE

Lemon meringue pie must equal apple pie in popularity. It is my favorite dessert pie and my Aunt Frances makes the absolute best in the world—tart and creamy with the perfect meringue top. I can still picture myself sitting at her kitchen table, rocking in a chair, licking my fingers, and longing for more.

PREHEAT OVEN: 400°F.

PASTRY NEEDED: Baked 9-inch pie shell.

BAKING TIME: Meringue top, 10 minutes at 400°F.

SERVINGS: 6 to 8.

  1½ **cups sugar**
    2 **tablespoons cornstarch**
    2 **tablespoons flour**
    ⅛ **teaspoon salt**
  1¾ **cups water**
      Juice of 1 lemon
      Grated rind of 1 lemon
    3 **egg yolks**
    4 **tablespoons unsalted (sweet) butter, cut into bits**
    1 **teaspoon vanilla**
      Aunt Frances' Never-Fail Meringue, page 27

Mix the sugar, cornstarch, flour, and salt together in a saucepan. Add the water and cook until thickened. Stir in the lemon juice and lemon rind. Mix a bit of the warm lemon mixture into egg yolks, then whisk this into remaining lemon mixture in saucepan. Add the butter and vanilla and beat until well blended and thick. Pour into prepared pie shell, cover with meringue, and bake according to directions on page 27.

BANANA CREAM PIE

Few restaurants prepare this all-time favorite from scratch, for instant puddings are simply too economical. Make it yourself to remember what a wonderful dessert it can be.

PASTRY NEEDED: Baked 9-inch traditional pie shell or any crumb crust.

SERVINGS: 6 to 8.

⅔ cup sugar
¼ cup cornstarch
3 egg yolks, lightly beaten
1½ cups milk
½ cup heavy cream
2 tablespoons unsalted (sweet) butter
¼ teaspoon vanilla
3 bananas
Whipped Cream Topping, page 26

Place sugar and cornstarch in a heavy saucepan and stir to blend. Add egg yolks, milk, and heavy cream and whisk over medium heat. Bring to a boil, stirring constantly, and boil for 1 minute. Remove from heat and whisk in butter and vanilla, mixing until butter has melted. Cover with wax paper and cool.

Slice bananas into bottom of prepared pie shell. Pour cooled custard over bananas and refrigerate for at least 1 hour. Cover with Whipped Cream Topping and refrigerate.

BERRY CREAM PIE

Use any fresh berries in this pie and adjust the sugar according to the sweetness of the berry.

PREHEAT OVEN: 425°F.

PASTRY NEEDED: Unbaked 9-inch pie shell.

BAKING TIME: 7 to 10 minutes at 425°F, 20 minutes at 325°F.

SERVINGS: 6 to 8.

1 cup sour cream
2 eggs
¾ cup sugar
1 tablespoon flour
1 teaspoon lemon juice
3½ cups fresh berries (blueberries, blackberries, strawberries, raspberries, boysenberries, dewberries, elderberries, or gooseberries)
Whipped Cream Topping, page 26

Beat the sour cream and eggs together in a medium-size mixing bowl. Blend in the sugar, flour, and lemon juice and lightly mix in the berries. Pour into pie shell and bake as directed above or until berries are set. Remove from oven, cool completely, and cover with Whipped Cream Topping, spreading it evenly with the tines of a fork or icing comb. Refrigerate until serving.

LEMON CREAM PIE

Lemony and creamy, tart and rich, and always a favorite. Limes, oranges, or tangerines can also be used.

PASTRY NEEDED: Baked 9-inch Chocolate Cookie Crumb Crust, page 25.

SERVINGS: 6 to 8.

4 tablespoons sugar
3 tablespoons cornstarch
1 cup milk
¾ cup heavy cream
2 eggs
1 tablespoon lemon juice
1 teaspoon grated lemon rind
2 tablespoons unsalted (sweet) butter, cut into bits
2 whole lemon, peeled, seeded, and cut into tiny segments (membranes removed)
Whipped Cream Topping, page 26

In a medium saucepan, mix the sugar and cornstarch together. Add the milk and heavy cream. Cook over medium heat until thick. Beat a little of the cream mixture into the eggs and quickly whisk this into the cream mixture in the saucepan. Add lemon juice, lemon rind, and butter and beat until butter is well blended. Stir in the bits of lemon and pour into prepared pie shell. Chill until well set, cover with Whipped Cream Topping, and serve immediately or refrigerate until ready to serve.

COCONUT CREAM PIE

You can, of course, substitute packaged prepared coconut for the fresh but the taste won't be the same. If you do use it, cut down on the amount of sugar. This pie is also good with a meringue topping in place of the suggested whipped cream.

PASTRY NEEDED: Baked 9-inch pie shell.

SERVINGS: 6 to 8.

¾ **cup sugar**
½ **cup cornstarch**
 1 **cup milk**
 1 **cup heavy cream**
 3 **large egg yolks**
1½ **cups grated fresh coconut**
 1 **teaspoon vanilla**
   Whipped Cream Topping, page 26
 1 **tablespoon grated fresh coconut**

Mix sugar and cornstarch together in a saucepan. Whip in the milk and heavy cream and cook over low to medium heat until mixture coats a spoon and begins to thicken. Do not let it brown. Whisk a little of the warm cream mixture into the egg yolks and then pour this back into the saucepan, beating rapidly. Stir in 1½ cups coconut and vanilla and cook for 2 or 3 minutes or until well blended. Cool slightly and pour into prepared pie shell. If using Whipped Cream Topping, refrigerate pie until well chilled, then decorate top with whipped cream and sprinkle with 1 tablespoon grated coconut. If using meringue, top with meringue immediately, sprinkle with 1 tablespoon grated coconut, and bake as directed on page 27. Cool before serving.

CHOCOLATE CREAM PIE

One of my childhood favorites, to which my mother often added walnuts. When I make it with water instead of milk, I add at least 1 egg yolk.

PASTRY NEEDED: Baked 9-inch traditional pie shell or any crumb crust.

SERVINGS: 6 to 8.

½ **cup sugar**
 2 **tablespoons flour**
 4 **tablespoons cocoa**
 2 **cups milk (or water, plus 1 egg yolk)**
 4 **tablespoons unsalted (sweet) butter, cut into bits**
   Whipped Cream Topping, page 26, or Aunt Frances' Never-Fail Meringue, page 27

Mix sugar, flour, and cocoa together in a saucepan and whisk in milk (or water plus egg yolk). Cook over medium heat until mixture coats a spoon and is thick. Beat in butter and pour into prepared pie shell. If topping with whipped cream, refrigerate pie until chilled and then cover with whipped cream. If topping with meringue, cover immediately with meringue and bake as directed on page 27.

IRISH COFFEE PIE

An extremely rich dessert. Serve with espresso after a simple meal.

PASTRY NEEDED: Baked 9-inch crumb crust, page 25.

SERVINGS: 6 to 8.

1¼ cups dark brown sugar
½ cup cornstarch
¼ cup flour
2 cups strong coffee
½ cup heavy cream
3 ounces unsweetened chocolate
½ cup unsalted (sweet) butter
3 egg yolks
¾ cup Irish whiskey
    Whipped Cream Topping, page 26

Mix the brown sugar, cornstarch, and flour together in a saucepan. Stir in 2 cups coffee and whisk until all corn-starch and flour is dissolved. Cook over medium heat until mixture begins to thicken and sugar is dissolved. Add heavy cream and remove from heat. Over medium heat melt the un-sweetened chocolate and butter together, pour into cream mixture, return to heat, and cook for about 2 minutes.

Whisk some of the chocolate mix-ture into the egg yolks, then pour this into the remaining chocolate mixture, whisking as you go. Stir in the Irish whiskey and continue stirring until mixture is well blended. Pour into prepared pie shell and chill until firm. Decorate top with Whipped Cream Topping and serve immedi-ately or refrigerate until ready to serve.

CHOCOLATE AND NUT

JENNY'S FUDGE PIE

Almost like candy. Easy to make and even easier to eat. My stepdaughter's answer to her chocolate craving.

PREHEAT OVEN: 450°F.

PASTRY NEEDED: Unbaked 9-inch pie shell.

BAKING TIME: 10 minutes at 450°F, 30 minutes at 325°F.

SERVINGS: 6 to 8.

6 tablespoons unsalted (sweet) butter
3 ounces unsweetened chocolate
4 eggs
1⅔ cups granulated sugar
½ cup brown sugar
1 teaspoon vanilla
1 cup chopped walnuts

Melt butter and chocolate together over very low heat and blend well. Remove from heat and let cool. Mix eggs, sugars, and vanilla together on medium speed of electric mixer until well blended. Stir in cooled chocolate mixture and walnuts. Pour in pie shell and bake as directed above or until fudge is set. Cool before serving.

CHOCOLATE WALNUT PIE

Just like fudge—rich in chocolate with a crunch of nuts.

PREHEAT OVEN: 375°F.

PASTRY NEEDED: Unbaked 9-inch double-crust pie.

BAKING TIME: 5 minutes at 375°F, 45 minutes at 325°F.

SERVINGS: 6 to 8.

- 4 eggs
- 1 cup light brown sugar
- ½ cup light corn syrup
- 4 tablespoons unsalted (sweet) butter, melted
- ½ cup flour
- 1½ cups semi-sweet chocolate bits
- 1½ cups whole walnuts

Beat eggs, brown sugar, and corn syrup together at medium speed of electric mixer. Add melted butter and flour and mix until well blended. Fold in chocolate bits and walnuts. Pour into pie shell and bake as directed above or until pie is set.

CHOCOLATE MOUSSE PIE

This spectacular chocolate pie is terrific for special dinners. It can be made ahead and frozen, then thawed and refrigerated on the day you need it.

PASTRY NEEDED: Baked 9-inch Chocolate Cookie Crumb Crust, page 25.

SERVINGS: 6 to 8.

- 6 ounces semi-sweet chocolate
- 2 ounces unsweetened chocolate
- 1 tablespoon unsalted (sweet) butter
- 2 tablespoons superfine sugar
- 3 egg yolks
- 3 egg whites, whipped to stiff but not dry peaks
- 1 cup heavy cream, whipped with 3 tablespoons confectioners' sugar
  Whipped Cream Topping, page 26

In the top of a double boiler put the chocolates, butter, and 2 tablespoons superfine sugar. Heat, stirring frequently, until chocolate is melted and sugar has dissolved. Remove from heat and gradually beat in egg yolks. Gently fold the whipped egg whites and whipped cream alternately into the chocolate mixture. Pour into prepared crumb crust, chill, and when pie is well set, pipe on a lattice top with the Whipped Cream Topping.

DERBYTOWN PIE

A pie traditionally associated with the running of the Kentucky Derby. Serve this at your next party and you'll be a sure winner.

PREHEAT OVEN: 350°F.

PASTRY NEEDED: Unbaked 9-inch pie shell.

BAKING TIME: 30 minutes at 350°F.

SERVINGS: 8 to 10.

- ½ cup unsalted (sweet) butter, melted
- 2 eggs
- 1 cup sugar
- ½ cup flour
- 1 cup semi-sweet chocolate bits
- 1½ cups chopped pecans
- 2 tablespoons bourbon

Cool butter and beat with eggs. Stir in sugar and flour and beat until well mixed. Fold in chocolate bits, nuts, and bourbon and pour in pie shell. Bake as directed above or until pie is set. May be served with whipped cream.

CHOCOLATE SILK PIE

A delicious pie that keeps well in the refrigerator. The nut crust adds a special crunch to the creamy chocolate.

PASTRY NEEDED: Baked 9-inch nut crust.

SERVINGS: 4 to 6.

¼ pound unsalted (sweet) butter
5 ounces unsweetened chocolate
¾ cup granulated sugar
3 eggs
1 tablespoon brandy
1 tablespoon orange juice
1 cup heavy cream
2 tablespoons confectioners' sugar
1 teaspoon brandy

In the top of a double boiler, melt the butter, chocolate, and granulated sugar. Heat, stirring frequently, until sugar is dissolved and mixture is well blended. Remove from heat and let cool. Beat eggs, 1 tablespoon brandy, and orange juice on medium speed. Gradually pour in the cooled chocolate mixture and beat until well blended. Pour into prepared crumb crust and chill. Whip heavy cream with confectioners' sugar and 1 teaspoon brandy and spread over well-chilled pie. Serve immediately or refrigerate until ready to serve.

Chocolate Silk Pie in a nut crust. Warning: Chocoholics will find this pie hard to resist!

COCONUT PECAN PIE

Fresh coconut and crunchy pecans combine to make an excellent pie.

PREHEAT OVEN: 375°F.

PASTRY NEEDED: Unbaked 9-inch pie shell.

BAKING TIME: 5 minutes at 375°F, 45 minutes at 325°F.

SERVINGS: 6 to 8.

¾ cup dark corn syrup
¾ cup sugar
2 tablespoons unsweetened cocoa
3 eggs
1 teaspoon vanilla
½ teaspoon grated orange rind
4 tablespoons unsalted (sweet) butter, melted
1½ cups pecans
1 cup grated coconut

Mix together all ingredients except pecans and coconut on medium speed of electric mixer, beating until well blended. Fold in pecans and coconut and pour into pie shell. Bake as directed above or until pie is well set.

MACADAMIA NUT PIE

Hawaii's version of the traditional Southern pecan pie. Delicious but expensive to make so save for a special occasion. Garnish with a dollop of whipped cream or sweetened sour cream.

PREHEAT OVEN: 400°F.

PASTRY NEEDED: Unbaked 9-inch pie shell.

BAKING TIME: 10 minutes at 400°F, 40 minutes at 325°F.

SERVINGS: 6 to 8.

⅔ cup light brown sugar
¾ cup light corn syrup
4 large eggs
4 tablespoons unsalted (sweet) butter, melted
1 tablespoon orange juice
1½ cups chopped macadamia nuts
½ cup whole macadamia nuts

Beat sugar, corn syrup, and eggs together at medium speed of electric mixer. Add cooled melted butter and orange juice and beat until well blended. Stir in chopped macadamia nuts and pour into pie shell. Arrange whole macadamia nuts on top and bake as directed above or until pie is set and golden.

VERMONT MAPLE NUT PIE

New England's version of pecan pie. The maple syrup adds a distinct flavor to the richness of the nuts. Top each serving with maple nut ice cream.

PREHEAT OVEN: 400°F.

PASTRY NEEDED: Unbaked 9-inch pie shell.

BAKING TIME: 10 minutes at 400°F, 25 minutes at 325°F.

SERVINGS: 6 to 8.

⅔ cup sugar

6 tablespoons unsalted (sweet) butter, melted and cooled

4 eggs

1 cup maple syrup

1 cup whole nuts (walnuts, pecans, or hazelnuts)

Mix all ingredients together until well blended. Pour into pie shell and bake as directed above or until pie is set and golden.

PEANUT PIE

I prefer unsalted peanuts for this pie, but it can be made with salted.

PREHEAT OVEN: 400°F.

PASTRY NEEDED: Unbaked 9-inch pie shell.

BAKING TIME: 10 minutes at 400°F, 25 minutes at 350°F.

SERVINGS: 6 to 8.

2 cups chopped unsalted peanuts (or salted, if desired)

3 eggs

1 cup dark corn syrup

1 cup light corn syrup

3 tablespoons unsalted (sweet) butter, melted and cooled

¼ cup peanut butter

Mix all ingredients together at medium speed of electric mixer. Pour into pie shell and bake as directed above or until pie is set.

MARYELLA'S PECAN PIE

Maryella Mixon has her own pecan trees in Georgia and she graciously sends pounds of her shelled fresh pecans to me each year. This pie has been named in gratitude for the great desserts she's helped me make. Very rich, so serve small slices.

PREHEAT OVEN: 350°F.

PASTRY NEEDED: Unbaked 9-inch pie shell.

BAKING TIME: 45 to 60 minutes at 350°F.

SERVINGS: 8 to 10.

1 cup sugar

1½ cups dark corn syrup

4 eggs

1 tablespoon flour

3 tablespoons unsalted (sweet) butter, melted

½ teaspoon grated lemon rind

1 teaspoon vanilla

1½ to 2 cups pecan halves

Mix together all ingredients except pecans at medium speed of electric mixer. Gently fold in pecans and pour into pie shell. Bake as directed above or until pie is golden. If pie begins to brown too quickly, lower heat to 325°F.

Maryella's Pecan Pie prepared with Mom's Flaky Pastry, and adorned with maple leaf cut-outs.

SOUSED PECAN PIE

A wonderful combination of rum, maple syrup, and nuts. Very, very rich so small servings are in order.

PREHEAT OVEN: 375°F.

PASTRY NEEDED: Unbaked 9-inch pie shell.

BAKING TIME: 5 minutes at 375°F, 45 minutes at 325°F

SERVINGS: 8 to 10.

½ cup sugar
½ cup unsalted (sweet) butter, cut into bits
3 eggs
½ cup maple syrup
½ cup light corn syrup
3 tablespoons rum
2 cups pecan halves

Beat the sugar and butter together at medium speed of electric mixer. Beat in eggs. Add maple and corn syrups and rum and beat until well blended. Fold in pecans and pour into pie shell. Bake as directed above or until pie is set.

WALNUT PIE

A spicy nut pie that can be enjoyed year round.

PREHEAT OVEN: 375°F.

PASTRY NEEDED: Unbaked 9-inch pie shell.

BAKING TIME: 10 minutes at 375°F, 45 minutes at 325°F.

SERVINGS: 6 to 8.

3 eggs
½ cup unsalted (sweet) butter, melted
¾ cup light brown sugar
½ cup light corn syrup
1 tablespoon ground cinnamon
¼ teaspoon ground nutmeg
¼ teaspoon ground cloves
Dash of ginger
2½ cups chopped walnuts

Mix together all ingredients except walnuts at medium speed of electric mixer. When well blended, stir in nuts. Pour into pie shell and bake as directed above or until pie is set.

UNUSUAL PIES

GREEN TOMATO PIE

Exotic but exquisite, this pie will never fail to surprise. It's fun to make simply because it is so different.

PREHEAT OVEN: 450°F.

PASTRY NEEDED: Unbaked 9-inch traditional or whole wheat double-crust pie.

BAKING TIME: 10 minutes at 450°F, 30 to 40 minutes at 350°F.

SERVINGS: 6 to 8.

6 cups peeled, sliced green tomatoes
1 tablespoon lemon juice
1 teaspoon ground cinnamon
1 teaspoon ground nutmeg
Dash of ground cloves
1 cup light brown sugar
¼ cup flour
2 tablespoons honey

Mix all ingredients together until well blended. Place in pie shell and finish with a lattice top as described on page 17. Bake as directed above or until pie bubbles and is golden.

BEAN PIE

*Often found on vegetarian menus.
If you lessen the sugar, you have an
interesting side dish for lunch.*

PREHEAT OVEN: 450°F.

PASTRY NEEDED: Unbaked 9-inch
traditional or whole wheat pie shell.

BAKING TIME: 10 minutes at 450°F,
40 minutes at 350°F.

SERVINGS: 6 to 8.

2½ cups mashed cooked navy
    beans
1½ cups sugar
2 tablespoons cornstarch
½ pound unsalted (sweet) butter,
    softened
4 eggs
1 13-ounce can evaporated milk
1 tablespoon lemon juice
1 tablespoon cinnamon

Beat all ingredients together at
medium speed of electric mixer. Pour
into pie shell and bake as directed
above or until pie is set.

SHAKER PIE

*This pie has often been called Maine
Lemon Pie, perhaps because of the Shaker
settlement at Sabbathday Lake.
The secret of its success is to use
very thin-skinned lemons and slice
them paper thin. Allow them to marinate
for at least 12 hours.*

PREHEAT OVEN: 450°F.

PASTRY NEEDED: Unbaked 9-inch
double-crust pie.

BAKING TIME: 10 minutes at 450°F,
30 minutes at 350°F.

SERVINGS: 6 to 8.

3 whole lemons, seeded and
    sliced paper thin
2½ cups superfine sugar
6 eggs, beaten

Mix the sliced lemons with the sugar,
cover, and refrigerate for at least 12
hours. Remove from refrigerator and
mix in beaten eggs. Pour into pie shell
and finish with lattice top as described
on page 17. Bake as directed above or
until golden.

SHOOFLY PIE

*A simple pie made by the Pennsylvania
Dutch and often served at breakfast.
One secret to its success is to work very
fast when mixing the molasses and soda.*

PREHEAT OVEN: 400°F.

PASTRY NEEDED: Unbaked 9-inch
pie shell.

BAKING TIME: 10 minutes at 400°F,
30 minutes at 350°F.

SERVINGS: 6 to 8.

1½ cups flour
¾ cup dark brown sugar
½ cup unsalted (sweet) butter, cut
    into bits
½ teaspoon baking soda
⅔ cup molasses
1 teaspoon baking soda
⅔ cup hot water

Mix the flour, brown sugar, butter,
and ½ teaspoon baking soda together
until crumbly. Set aside. Quickly combine the molasses, 1 teaspoon baking
soda, and hot water. Pour immediately
into the flour mixture, stir to blend,
and pour into pie shell. Bake as directed
above or until pie is set.

BLACK BOTTOM PIE

A terrific combination of chocolate and lemon, sweet and tart. One of my favorite company desserts.

PASTRY NEEDED: Baked 9-inch traditional pie shell or crumb crust.

SERVINGS: 8 to 10.

½ **cup semi-sweet chocolate bits**
4 **eggs**
½ **cup sugar**
¾ **cup unsalted (sweet) butter, cut into bits**
½ **cup lemon juice**
  Whipped Cream Topping, page 26
  Chocolate sprinkles, curls, or grated semi-sweet chocolate

Melt the chocolate bits over hot water. Pour into pie shell and spread all over the bottom and up the sides. Let cool and set. Try to get an even coating on pie shell.

With an electric mixer, whip the eggs and sugar until well blended. Stir in the butter and then the lemon juice. Pour into small heavy saucepan and, over medium heat, bring to a boil, stirring constantly. As soon as mixture boils remove from heat and stir to cool it down a bit. Pour into chocolate-coated pie shell, refrigerate for about 1 hour, and cover with Whipped Cream Topping. Sprinkle chocolate over the whipped cream and refrigerate until ready to serve.

SPONGE PIE

Light and cakelike, Sponge Pie is a pleasant dessert after a heavy meal.

PREHEAT OVEN: 400°F.

PASTRY NEEDED: Unbaked 9-inch pie shell.

BAKING TIME: 10 minutes at 400°F, 40 minutes at 300°F.

SERVINGS: 6 to 8.

¼ **cup unsalted (sweet) butter, softened**
1 **cup granulated sugar**
4 **egg yolks**
4 **tablespoons flour**
1½ **cups milk**
⅓ **cup lemon juice**
1 **tablespoon grated lemon rind**
4 **egg whites**
2 **tablespoons superfine sugar**

Cream the butter, granulated sugar, egg yolks, and flour together at medium speed of electric mixer. Add the milk, lemon juice, and rind and mix until well blended. Beat egg whites with superfine sugar until stiff and fold into mixture. Pour into pie shell and bake as directed above or until pie is set.

Black Bottom Pie made with Mom's Flaky Pastry, dressed up with whipped cream, chocolate bits, and a distinctive trim.

Chapter

TARTS,
TURNOVERS,
FRIED PIES,
AND DUMPLINGS

Five

FRUIT TARTS

These are the tarts that you see on pastry trays in restaurants. You can use canned fruit that has been well drained, but they are always best with fresh fruit. These do not keep well so make just enough for immediate use.

PASTRY NEEDED: 10 baked tart shells.

SERVINGS: 10 tarts.

4 large egg yolks
1 cup sugar
3 tablespoons cornstarch
2 cups hot milk
2 tablespoons vanilla
2 cups fresh fruit, washed, seeded, and sliced if necessary
½ cup currant or apple jelly

Beat egg yolks until very thick. Gradually add sugar and keep beating until a ribbon forms when you lift the beaters. Gradually add cornstarch and beat to blend. Slowly add hot milk, beating constantly. Pour mixture into saucepan and cook, stirring constantly, over medium heat until mixture is slightly thick. Do not let it burn. Remove from heat, whisk in vanilla, and chill for about 30 minutes.

Fill tart shells two-thirds full with chilled pastry cream and arrange prepared fruit on top in an attractive pattern. Melt the jelly over low heat and spoon on top of fruit in each tart. Refrigerate until ready to serve.

CHESS TARTS

I had heard of chess tarts long before I tasted one. As with chess pies, there seem to be hundreds of recipes for them. Some are dressed up with raisins and nuts, others are plain and simple. This recipe is one I've developed by taking a bit of all the chess tart recipes that have been passed along to me.

PREHEAT OVEN: 375°F.

PASTRY NEEDED: 10 unbaked tart shells.

BAKING TIME: 10 minutes at 375°F, 30 minutes at 325°F.

YIELD: 10 tarts.

4 eggs
1½ cups light brown sugar
½ cup dark brown sugar
2 tablespoons flour
6 tablespoons unsalted (sweet) butter, melted
1 tablespoon vinegar
¼ cup heavy cream
1 teaspoon grated lemon rind
10 nut halves

Beat together all but last ingredient at medium speed of electric mixer. Pour into tart shells. Top each with a nut half and bake as directed above or until fillings are set. Cool before serving.

LEMON TARTS

These tart tarts are an English favorite. Called lemon curd in Great Britain, the filling is also used as a spread on scones or toast.

PASTRY NEEDED: 10 baked tart shells.

YIELD: 10 tarts.

3 whole eggs
2 egg yolks
1½ cups sugar
1½ cups unsalted (sweet) butter, melted
½ cup lemon juice
1 tablespoon grated lemon rind
Whipped Cream Topping, page 26
10 very thin slices of lemon for garnish

Beat the eggs, egg yolks, and sugar together in a saucepan until well mixed and thick. You'll have a creamy, light yellow, well-blended mixture. Add the cooled melted butter, lemon juice, and rind and cook over medium heat until thick. Remove from heat, cover, and chill. Place an equal amount of lemon filling in each baked tart shell. Top with whipped cream and garnish with lemon slice. Serve immediately.

A colorful assortment of Fruit Tarts baked in Tart Crust, topped with strawberries, raspberries, blood oranges, kiwis, and mixed fruits— something for everyone.

CHOCOLATE TARTS

Miniature chocolate cream pies.

PASTRY NEEDED: 10 baked tart shells.

YIELD: 10 tarts.

½ cup granulated sugar
2 tablespoons flour
4 tablespoons unsweetened cocoa
2 cups milk
4 tablespoons unsalted (sweet) butter, cut into bits
1 cup very cold heavy cream
2 tablespoons confectioners' or superfine sugar
Pinch of cream of tartar
Chocolate sprinkles

Mix granulated sugar, flour, and cocoa together in a saucepan and whisk in milk. Cook over medium heat until mixture coats a spoon and is thick. Beat in butter and cool.

In chilled bowl and using chilled beaters, whip cold heavy cream. As it begins to thicken, add confectioners' or superfine sugar and cream of tartar. Continue beating at high speed until cream is stiff and holds a peak.

Fill each tart shell with chocolate mixture and top with whipped cream and chocolate sprinkles. Refrigerate until ready to serve.

BERRY TARTS

Similar to cheesecake. Use any berry that is in season but these tarts are especially good with strawberries or blueberries.

PASTRY NEEDED: 10 baked tart shells.

SERVINGS: 10 tarts.

1 cup cream cheese, softened
½ cup milk
4 tablespoons superfine sugar
2 cups whole berries
½ cup currant jelly, melted

Beat the cream cheese, milk, and sugar together until light and airy. Spoon a small amount into the bottom of each tart shell and arrange berries in a pattern on top. Pour melted jelly on top of each tart and refrigerate until ready to serve.

FRUIT TURNOVERS

Any fresh fruit will make a tasty filling. Turnovers may be served warm or cold, with ice cream or whipped cream. They are great tucked into a lunch box, too.

PREHEAT OVEN: 400°F.

PASTRY NEEDED: Ten 4½-inch pastry rounds (made from traditional, whole wheat, or butter pastry recipe for 9-inch double-crust pie).

BAKING TIME: 20 to 25 minutes at 400°F.

YIELD: 10 turnovers.

2 cups peeled, cored, and chopped apples, peaches, pears, or any other fruit
⅓ cup sugar
1 tablespoon lemon juice
1 tablespoon flour
1 teaspoon ground cinnamon
¼ cup unsalted (sweet) butter, cut into bits
¼ teaspoon ground nutmeg (for apple turnovers)

Mix all ingredients together. Place a tablespoon of filling in center of each round, moisten edges of rounds with water, fold in half, and seal with fork tines or fingers. Brush with milk, and prick steam holes in the top of each. Bake as directed above or until golden. You may wish to sprinkle them with confectioners' sugar while they are still warm.

APPLESAUCE TURNOVERS

Just about any kind of fruit sauce can be used in these. Homemade is always best but prepared will work in a pinch.

PREHEAT OVEN: 400°F.

PASTRY NEEDED: Ten 4½-inch pastry rounds (made from traditional, whole wheat, or butter pastry recipe for 9-inch double-crust pie).

BAKING TIME: 15 to 20 minutes at 400°F.

YIELD: 10 turnovers.

1½ cups homemade applesauce
½ cup raisins
½ cup chopped walnuts
½ teaspoon cinnamon

Mix all ingredients together. Place a tablespoon of filling in center of each round, moisten edges of rounds with water, fold in half, and seal with fork tines or fingers. Brush with milk and prick steam holes in the top of each. Bake as directed above or until golden and sprinkle with confectioners' sugar while they are still warm.

VARIATION

JAM TURNOVERS

Use your favorite jam in place of ingredients above. Spoon a tablespoon of jam in center of each pastry round and proceed as described above.

FRIED PIES

Fried pies are traditionally made with cooked dried fruit as filling. You can use prunes, apples, apricots, or peaches, alone or in combination. You will need a deep-fat fryer or heavy skillet holding melted vegetable shortening ¾" deep and heated to 375°F.

PASTRY NEEDED: Ten 4½-inch pastry rounds.

COOKING TIME: About 4 minutes.

YIELD: 10 pies.

2 cups chopped dried fruit
   Hot water
½ cup sugar
1 teaspoon cinnamon
1 tablespoon butter
¼ cup confectioners' sugar

Cover the chopped dried fruit with hot water and let sit for about 10 minutes. Add sugar and cinnamon, stir until sugar is dissolved, and let sit an additional 5 minutes. Drain off excess water. Stir in butter. Place tablespoon of filling in center of pastry round, moisten edges of round with water, and fold in half. Seal with fork tines or fingers, being particularly sure that the edges are pressed firmly together. Place in hot fat and fry for about 4 minutes or until golden. (Don't fry too many at a time.) Remove from heat, drain on paper towels, and sprinkle with confectioners' sugar while warm.

DUMPLINGS

An easy dessert that sometimes is used for a hearty breakfast. Not too sweet but very satisfying. You can obviously make as many or as few as you wish. One 9-inch double-crust pie recipe should be sufficient to cover 6 medium-size baking apples or 8 medium-size pears.

PREHEAT OVEN: 450°F.

PASTRY NEEDED: Unbaked 9-inch double-crust pie recipe cut into 6 or 8 circles, each large enough to enclose an apple or pear.

BAKING TIME: 10 minutes at 450°F, 30 minutes at 350°F.

SERVINGS: 6 or 8.

6 **medium-size baking apples or**
   8 **medium-size Bosc or winter**
   pears
¾ **cup cinnamon-sugar mixture,**
   approximately (¾ cup sugar
   mixed with 1 tablespoon
   cinnamon)
½ **cup raisins (optional)**
¼ **cup chopped nuts (optional)**
6 **or 8 tablespoons butter**
   Heavy cream

Core each piece of fruit and cut off a 1-inch-wide strip of peel around the top. Set fruit in center of pastry circle and bring dough up around the fruit, leaving the peeled top open. Pleat pastry if necessary to make a tight fit, and press pastry against fruit. Fill the fruit cavity about half full with the cinnamon-sugar mixture. If desired, add a few raisins and some chopped nuts. Put 1 tablespoon butter on top of each dumpling and place in individual baking dishes. Bake as directed above or until pastry is golden and fruit is tender but not falling apart. Serve with heavy cream while still warm.

SOURCES

Chicken-In-Every Potpie, page 30: All bowls, The Broadway Panhandler; cooling rack and dish towel, Williams-Sonoma.

Brunswick Chicken, page 34: Pie server and napkin, Williams-Sonoma; glass, Pottery Barn.

Chili con Carne, page 44: All pottery, Bennington Pottery; napkin, ABC Carpet & Home.

Veal & Peppers, page 52: Pie pan, Dean & DeLuca; pie server, Pottery Barn.

Pissaladière, page 56: Glass, Pottery Barn.

Nirvana, page 61: Pitcher, Macy's; star plate, Fishs Eddy; spatula, Zona; pie plate, Williams-Sonoma.

Quiche, page 65: Large glass plate, Zona; flatware, Pottery Barn; napkin, ABC Carpet & Home.

Mom's Apple Pie, page 74: Plate, cup and saucer, Williams-Sonoma; napkin, ABC Carpet & Home.

Peach Blueberry, page 80: Pitcher, Williams-Sonoma.

Chocolate Cheese, page 94: Bowl and plates, Zona; pie server, Bloomingdale's; flatware, Pottery Barn.

Coconut Custard, page 99: Flatware, glass, and plate, Pottery Barn.

Chocolate Silk, page 108: Flatware, Williams-Sonoma.

Maryella's Pecan, page 111: Pie plate, Dean & DeLuca.

Black Bottom, page 114: Plates, cup and saucer, Williams-Sonoma; flatware, Pottery Barn.

Tarts, page 119: Glass, Pottery Barn; bowl, Zona.

SUPPLIERS

ABC Carpet & Home
888 Broadway
New York, NY 10003
(212) 473-3000

Bennington Potters, Inc.
324 County Street
Bennington, VT 05201-0199
(802) 447-7531

Bloomingdale's
1000 3rd Avenue
New York, NY 10022
(212) 705-2000

The Broadway Panhandler
520 Broadway
New York, NY 10012
(212) 966-3434

Dean & DeLuca Inc.
560 Broadway
New York, NY 10012
(212) 431-1691

Fishs Eddy
889 Broadway
New York, NY 10003
(212) 420-9020

Macy's
151 West 34th Street
New York, NY 10001
(212) 695-4400

The Pottery Barn
700 Broadway
New York, NY 10012
(212) 505-6377

Williams-Sonoma
20 East 60th Street
New York, NY 10022
(212) 980-5155

Zona
97 Greene Street
New York, NY 10012
(212) 925-6750

INDEX

KITCHEN METRICS

The table gives approximate, rather than exact, conversions.

Spoons

¼ teaspoon   =   1 milliliter
½ teaspoon   =   2 milliliters
1 teaspoon   =   5 milliliters
1 tablespoon = 15 milliliters
2 tablespoons = 25 milliliters
3 tablespoons = 50 milliliters

Cups

¼ cup =   50 milliliters
⅓ cup =   75 milliliters
½ cup = 125 milliliters
⅔ cup = 150 milliliters
¾ cup = 175 milliliters
1 cup = 250 milliliters

Oven Temperatures

200°F = 100°C
225°F = 110°C
250°F = 120°C
275°F = 140°C
300°F = 150°C
325°F = 160°C
350°F = 180°C
375°F = 190°C
400°F = 200°C
425°F = 220°C
450°F = 230°C
475°F = 240°C